The
Senior
Software
Engineer

11 Practices of an Effective Technical Leader

by David Bryant Copeland

Contents

Acknowledgements

Thanks to my wife, Amy, for giving me the space, time, and encouragement to work on this book (as well as her keen copyrighting skills).

I'd also like to thank the amazing developers I've worked with over the years including Jeff Barrett, Thomas Copeland, Patrick Joyce, Jeff Kolesky, and Tom Vaughan, who were kind enough to review a draft of this book. Also, thanks to Adam Morse who designed and build the book's website (as well as encouraged me to learn about typography before typesetting this book).

1

Welcome to Your New Career

Welcome to the start of a what I hope will be an exciting, enlightening journey that takes you from competent code monkey to truly senior developer. At the end, you'll be in charge of your own destiny, able to work with everyone on your team, and even lead them to deliver huge value to your company or organization. The key isn't some new framework or programming language, but to fully embrace the position of software engineer as something more than just writing code.

Don't get me wrong - this isn't a book about being a middle manager of a software team. It's a book about all the skills you never realized you needed to cultivate when writing code. Skills like working well with others who have different priorities than you. Skills like writing. Skills like leading a team without giving up writing code.

At the time of this writing, I've been a professional programmer for over 18 years. I've worked for product companies, both consumer and enterprise. I've been a consultant. I've been a government contractor. I've worked as part of a 3 person team at a startup, and a 100+ person distributed team at a large multi-national company. And it wasn't until 2012-16 years in-that I truly understood what a senior software engineer really is.

In most companies, "senior" typically refers to a rank within the company. A senior analyst "outranks" a junior analyst: they get to make more decisions and, at least on paper, have more control over the direction of the work being done.

In our field, "senior" usually means you have about three years of experience, or did a good job negotiating a title when applying for work. The result is that most developers at most companies have "senior" in their title. I've had "senior" (or better) in my title for most of my career.

Programmers tend to be a merit-based bunch, and the product of our work - computer programs - are far more objective than what most other people produce at their jobs. Because of this, implicit leaders will emerge amongst a group of "senior" developers. Job titles rarely reflect who has the most respect, or who can be trusted with the most important tasks. What took me so long to learn was that that trust and respect isn't borne entirely of programming ability, but of a well-roundedness that can be difficult to quantify.

To be a trusted, respected developer, who's rightfully seen as a leader, requires more than just coding chops. It requires a higher-level view of the purpose and function of software engineering in most organizations, and a dedication to that purpose. The purpose, of course, is simple: deliver results with software.

In many organizations, "someone else" figures out what the company needs and then directs the developers to deliver something that should meet those needs. While this seems logical, the best developers I know don't entirely rely on this. They instead align themselves to the company's needs, rather than wait around for instructions on how to meet them.

These developers aren't stuck in management, either. They code, and they usually work on the most important, most challenging, or most fun aspects of the systems they create. These developers, by making their organization's goals *their* goals, have control over their careers, and earn trust and respect, through simple demonstration of ability. Put simply, they get the best jobs.

This book will outline ten major areas of your career to cultivate. Primarily, each chapter is designed to express the importance of that area to you as a developer. Each chapter also contains specific information on how to develop your skills in these areas, often very prescriptive. These instructions aren't the only way to develop your abilities, but they will serve you well if you find yourself overwhelmed by the task of, say, convincing your non-technical boss to use some new framework.

Each skill we'll discuss builds on the skills previous. As such, we'll start out where we're comfortable: coding. We'll outline a simple and effective personal process for fixing bugs that works in any environment before expanding on that process to include implementing major features in existing systems.

Next, we'll enter the realm of personal interaction. We'll start by talking about technical debt and sloppy code, since these have the biggest effect on software that's visible to the non-technical outside world. Next, we'll talk about working effectively with all sorts of different people, which is so important, yet can be so difficult.

The second half of the book is a course toward being a true leader. We start with making technical decisions and arguments amidst a wash of conflicting priorities - a skill you'll need later when we learn how to successfully bootstrap a new application. Successfully creating an app from nothing requires the ability to write effectively, and we'll discuss that as well.

The last three chapters are about building, being a responsive part of, and ultimately leading a team. We'll learn how to conduct a technical interview, manage our time without getting lost in the code and finish the book with a whirlwind tour of a technical lead's responsibilities throughout the life-cycle of an application, from starting it off, to delivering it, to leaving it behind.

For the second addition, I've also included three new essays on being a senior software engineer. "Engineer As Product Manager" encourages you to take an active interest in the business you're a part of. "Production is All That Matters" discusses the importance of running software and how you should take a strong interest in how yours behaves. "Responsible Refactoring" expands on this to talk about how important it is to stop fiddling with working code, and how to know when a re-design is the right thing to do.

But first, we need to talk more about aligning your goals with those of your company. We need to shift our thinking from coding up features to a focus on delivering results in everything we do.

2

Focus on Delivering Results

A senior software engineer is trusted and expected to do the most important work and to do it reliably. The way to accomplish that is to focus everything you do on the delivery of *results*.

At a previous job, I was responsible for the purchasing and refund logic of a large e-commerce website. One day, Mary (one of our customer service representatives) emailed me with a problem. Mary was attempting to refund a customer but the system wouldn't let her, instead giving her a cryptic error message.

I didn't immediately know what was wrong, so I was about to write her back with the message "I'll look into it", but I stopped. What value would Mary get out of such an email? What purpose would it serve to send her a promise, but no real answer? I decided that she deserved exactly one response from me: an email with a definitive answer in it.

I did some research and realized that a constraint of our credit card processor was preventing the type of refund she was attempting. She would have to wait 24 hours from the time of purchase for the refund to go through.

I made a small change to detect this special case and show a more helpful error message. I deployed the change and wrote Mary back with my findings. I explained that, while there was no way to avoid the 24 hour waiting period, she would at least get a more instructive error message in the future.

She sent me a problem and I replied with a solution.

After this, I began to approach *every* task this way. Instead of making promises or publicizing plans, I resolved to focus on delivering results - and results only - as much as I possibly could. I wanted everything that I produced to be a definitive answer or working code or both.

You must make this change as well. By focusing on the delivery of results, you will become more reliable and your work product will be of much higher value to the company (or yourself).

You might think that the phrase "focus on delivering results" is a simple sound-bite or that you already take a "results-oriented" approach. I used to think this too, but the *results* and *focus* I'm talking about are more specific, more literal. Let's first understand these two terms and then see how this will change the way we work.

2.1 Results

On any reasonably-sized software project, there are a lot of *deliverables* however few of these are what I would call a *result*. Most teams have some sort of project manager whose function is to keep the team moving, often by facilitating a process for development. To do this, a good project manager will use various tools and techniques such as project plans, estimates, and delivery schedules.

While these are useful, they are fundamentally different from working software and it's important that you and your team understand the difference. Your company's customers don't pay for project roadmaps. Users cannot get their work done with a project schedule or burn-down chart. Working, shipped software is what pays the bills and solves users' problems.

Of course, shipped code isn't necessarily a result. A result from shipped code is one that causes a positive change in how the business works. Code that doesn't have a measurable impact on the application it's a part of is not nearly as important as code that does.

Results are more than just working software, however. As my anecdote above demonstrates, sometimes a result is as simple as a definitive answer to a question. An explanation about how something works is supremely useful, whereas an email that you'll "look into it" is not.

A *result* then, is an artifact of direct business value. Working code, documentation, and definitive statements are all results. Anything else must be understood as fundamentally different.

This isn't to say that project schedules, status reports, and other similar "deliverables" have no value. You just need to treat them as a *means* to an end, not an end unto themselves. If you start treating *progress* toward a goal as being just as acceptable as actually *achieving* said goal, you or your team will lose focus and momentum, and be less and less valuable to the company over time.

Now that we understand what a result is, let's talk about what it means to truly *focus* on its delivery.

2.2 Focus

The applicable definition of focus is "the act of concentrating interest or activity on something". As a developer, you know how important focus is. Certain coding tasks would be impossible if you were unable to focus. This focus however, comes with a price. It requires that you ignore or dismiss other things around you. You need to apply all of your brainpower to the task at hand.

Focusing on results means that you apply this focus to every aspect of your job. When you know the results you must deliver, anything that takes your focus away has the potential to put that result at risk, and reduce the value of what you're delivering to the company.

The classic example of this is the micro-manager. Such a person hovers over their subordinates, constantly checking in and requesting status reports. This causes his team to lose their focus and deliver less value overall than if the manager had just left them alone.

Of course, you can lose focus all on your own, either by multi-tasking or by attending to tasks unrelated to the results you're working hard to deliver. Even the smallest thing can distract you.

For example, responding to Mary's email immediately, even if just to say "I'll check it out", is a distraction. By waiting a bit, I was able to keep my focus on what I was doing. Further, by not promising Mary anything initially, my ability to continue to deliver results was not affected. Finally, by actually delivering her a result in the end, she has no motivation to come over and interrupt me - an all-too-familiar distraction - because she knows that emails to me get results.

If something more urgent came up, I could forward her email to someone else, or simply look into it later. In the worst case, I could simply respond that I didn't have time to look into it. That wouldn't be ideal, but it would be fair. An unfulfilled promise to look into it wouldn't be.

Part of focus is keeping your promises to a minimum. A promise to do something now can put you into a bind later. If delivering on your promise takes you away from delivering results, you either need to break your promise or delay delivering valuable results (which themselves might've been previously promised). Neither option is a good one.

This isn't to say you should never promise anything - the company deserves to know what you're working on and when it might be available, but you need to start treating promises literally. If you promise something, even implicitly, you *have* to deliver on it.

Focusing your work on delivering results does have one potential drawback. Since you will be making fewer promises (such as incremental delivery schedules), and you'll be minimizing non-results (like progress reports), it can be hard to tell the difference between actually making progress and being stalled. It can also be hard for project stakeholders to feel comfortable that you'll meet your estimated delivery dates.

The way to deal with this is to move away from large projects. Work in small chunks that deliver useful results frequently. In effect, you'll turn status reports into deliverable business value.

2.3   Deliver Smaller Results More Often

It's hard to estimate large projects and it's hard to convey how much progress is being made on them at any given time. Taking on a project like this puts you in an awkward position, because you'll be expected to ultimately make promises you aren't sure you'll be able to keep.

What tends to happen is that everyone agrees that your "ball-park estimate" is just that, and not a reasonable deadline, but you end up being held to it nevertheless. You've made an implicit promise and can be seen as unreliable. Further, providing progress reports like "75% done" implies a level of accuracy in project tracking that is typically not possible.

By not reporting progress between deliveries, your project will lack visibility. If you're given a three month time-table to deliver, that's three months of stakeholders being entirely in the dark. To deal with this, you should re-imagine your project as a series of small results-driven deliverables. Deliver working software as frequently as you can. Reduce the scope of your project to the absolute bare minimum needed to solve the *business* problem at hand, and deliver that as soon as possible.

Doing this has two advantages. First, it turns a boring progress report into working, usable software. You won't have to merely *tell* the rest of the company how far along you are, you can *show* them. Secondly, promises of smaller value over shorter time are easier to keep. You are much more likely to accurately estimate one week's worth of work than you are one month's.

This isn't a radical idea; it's the basis of agile software development. The reason I've avoided the term until now is to emphasize that your goal should be delivering results, not following some particular development process. Story cards, sprints, and stand-up meetings are not ends unto themselves. If they are roadblocks to delivering results, they must go. That being said, project planning tools like story cards or schedules can be useful. Techniques such as stand-up meetings and status reports do have their place, as long as they are used internally and don't take your focus off the results you need to deliver.

2.4 Plans, Schedules, and Status Reports

Apple is renowned for never publicly promising any product that isn't shipping. Apple doesn't demo works in progress, nor do they promise any feature that isn't ready for customers to buy. This doesn't mean they don't plan and track their progress, however. They simply choose not to expose it publicly, which makes them appear highly organized and very reliable.

Think of yourself, your team, and your company as an onion. You're at the center and each layer represents the larger structure of which you are a part. Each layer delivers results - and only results - to the layer around it. Inside, however, planning, tracking, processes, and other tools for delivery can (and should be) used. But they are used *privately* as internal tools. They should rarely be exposed to the outside world, because they have the potential to lead to broken promises, either through misinterpretation or over-zealous project management.

There are times when it may be appropriate to "pull back the curtain" and expose your internal processes to the outside. Often, requirements are driven by a complex set of priorities and you or your team might be only a small part of a larger commitment. In that case, you may need to communicate details of your progress to those relying on your team. Just keep in mind that a broken promise is often worse than no promise. Peel the onion's layers with care.

The majority of this book is focused on the center of the onion: you. We'll talk about how you can plan and conduct your work so that you become a developer delivering nothing but result after result: a *senior* developer. You won't burden your co-workers with vague progress reports, nor will you be seen as unreliable by making promises you can't keep. Instead, you'll be seen as effective, thorough, reliable, and valuable, because you'll be focused on results (and you'll plan to deliver those results frequently).

2.5 Moving On

I never truly understood what a focus on results really was until I was in an environment that encouraged it. It gave me a whole new perspective on many jobs I've had and shed a lot of light on my successes (and failures) over the years. Everything that follows flows from this focus on results.

At times, you'll encounter roadblocks that stand between you and delivering valuable results to the business. Sometimes, you can work around them, and sometimes you'll need to compromise. We'll call out common issues and talk about how to work around them, but there will be occasions where your team or company stand in direct opposition to delivering the valuable results they so crave.

It's these times when you have to remember the most important result on which to focus: your career. If you find yourself unable to focus on delivering results it may be worth considering if you're in the right job. Some work environments are not designed to allow you to thrive.

Make this decision with care. It's often possible to make improvements by showing how better practices deliver better results; that's the theme of this book. We'll talk about common roadblocks along the way and some simple workarounds. In the end, you must decide for yourself how much you are willing to compromise.

Now that we have a context for where we're going, let's start getting there. Our first step is going to be fixing bugs and building small enhancements, which is often the first step in a career *or* in a new job.

3

Fix Bugs Efficiently and Cleanly

No matter your experience level, the first task you're given at a new job is likely to fix a bug or implement a very minor feature in an existing application. When you are just starting out in your career this will likely be your primary job.

The reason is that fixing bugs or implementing small features is typically straightforward, can be completed in a day or two, and doesn't require an in-depth understanding of the business or codebase.

Even though these tasks are small, they aren't unimportant. The smallest changes in software can sometimes make a user's life markedly easier. These tasks are also an easy way to deliver results quickly, and are a perfect place to begin honing your personal software development process.

In this chapter, I'll show you a basic process for fixing bugs or implementing small features that you can use on any small task in any company with any technology stack. The process is based around the theory of Test-Driven Development

(TDD), with its focus being on pragmatism, efficiency, and - you guessed it - results.

3.1 Overview

First, it's important to understand why you even *need* a defined process. Such a process allows you to focus on the right thing at the right time. When you're working, you don't want to wrestle with how to approach your work or what the next thing to do is. You want your head in the *problem you're solving*. By learning and following a formalized process, you free your mind to focus only on the work: the machinations of solving the problem and checking that it's correct become rote.

Further, by following the same process every time your productivity and quality become more predictable. The more predictable you are, the better you will be at estimating how long something will take and the more promises you can make about your work.

The process you'll want to follow is five simple steps:

1. Understand the problem.

2. Write tests that fail (because the problem has yet to be solved).

3. Solve the problem as quickly as you can, using your tests to know when you've solved it.

4. Modify your solution for readability, conciseness, and safety by using your tests to make sure you haven't broken anything.

5. Commit your changes.

These are the only steps you need and they are ordered explicitly to achieve the desired results: a correct and maintainable solution. We'll delve into each one in a moment, but this process encourages two things:

- Thinking before coding

- Separating "getting it to work" from "doing it right". It's hard to do both at the same time.

If you're familiar with TDD, you'll notice that steps 2, 3, and 4 are the classic "red/green/refactor" cycle recommended by that approach. If you are skeptical of working this way, please bear with me. I have a practical reason for suggesting it. The additional steps - 1 and 5 - are equally important as they represent the way in which you connect to the world outside of just coding.

Let's go over each step one at a time. For each step, we'll talk about some common roadblocks you might hit and some suggestions for working around them. Finally, we'll see an example of this process in action.

3.2 Understand the Problem

Most developers enjoy programming and when faced with a task, are eager to start coding. Coding is how we solve problems so we tend to want to take the quickest route we can to start coding. Modern "agile" development methodologies encourage this with mantras like "No Big Design Up Front". Many developer-centric companies appear to encourage this as well. In his letter to potential shareholders of Facebook, Mark Zuckerberg included an essay entitled "The Hacker Way" which contained the phrase "code wins arguments".

These notions are very much in line with our focus on delivering results, however they can often be misinterpreted as "just start coding".

By rushing into coding up a solution, you run the risk of solving the wrong problem, or wasting time pursuing a partial solution. Any work you do to solve the wrong problem is wasted effort that must be undone. Further, the amount of time required to re-do the work later is orders of magnitude higher than taking a bit of time now to understand what you need to do.

These issues can easily be addressed by taking a breath and *thinking* for a few moments. "No Big Design Up Front" doesn't mean "No Design" any more than "code wins arguments" means "coding is the only activity worth doing".

If you're fixing a bug, the easiest way to understand the problem is to actually *use* the buggy software and see the problem yourself. Even if you think you know the exact line of code where the problem occurs, actually seeing the bug as a user would can be hugely insightful. It may turn out that the line of code you thought you'd have to change is perfectly correct and some *other* part of the system is doing something wrong.

If you're making a very small feature, use the application in a way that reveals the missing feature. Navigate to the proper screen (or go to the right page) and spend five minutes talking with a project stakeholder about how the feature should work (even if you have been given detailed documentation about it). A human conversation can reveal volumes of information that isn't present in a document.

Once you've done this, take a quick trip through the source code and plot out - in your mind or on paper - how you're going to solve the problem. What do you need to do to know that you're done? What parts of the system will need to change? Do you understand each of these parts enough to confidently change them? What's the test coverage like? Can you be sure you won't introduce a regression bug?

For such small tasks, answering these questions shouldn't take much time, especially on a codebase you understand. For a codebase you *don't* understand it's even more crucial to actually take the time to plan your solution.

What you need to resist is the urge to "fix everything" you find along the way. Remember to maintain your focus. You are fixing a bug or adding a feature that address the specific problem you've just uncovered. Any work that's not directly related to that is a potential distraction. Refactor poorly-designed code later.

At this point, you should have a solid understanding of the problem you need to solve, and a general approach to doing so. You will have spent hopefully less than an hour, possibly even just a few minutes. If it *does* take longer, it could indicate the problem is more complex than initially thought (and thus validate the extra care you are taking before coding).

Roadblocks

Misunderstanding the problem.

When you are new to a domain, or when a domain is particularly complex, it can be often be difficult to truly understand the problem. Worse, you might only *think* you understand the problem but don't. This will result in doing work that must be re-done.

The best way to deal with this is to "play back" your understanding the stakeholders. If the underlying business problem is complex, try to walk through it slowly and take more time. Verbalizing your understanding back to the stakeholder is often the quickest way to making sure you are both on the same page.

No access to the production system.

17

It's unfortunately common for developers to not have any access to actually *use* the production system. This makes it difficult to see a bug in action or visualize where a new feature will be added.

If this is the case, try to find someone who *does* have production access and ask them nicely to give you a demo of the problem. If you can't sit at their desk and watch, suggest having them record a short screencast and emailing it to you. There are several free web-based screencasting services that make this very simple. Screenshots of the bug can work as well.

It may be that the culture of your organization makes it too difficult (or impossible) to view the production application. In this case you'll have to recreate the issue in your development environment. This isn't ideal, but it's the best you can do.

No access to project stakeholders.

A more likely scenario is that you simply don't have access to the stakeholders of the project. In other words, you can't have your five minute discussion about the system with the person who either noticed the problem or requested the feature.

In this case, you need to have this conversation with *someone*, so find the closest person you can to the project stakeholder. This might be your team lead or project manager. Hopefully, one of them understands the issue well enough to help you fully understand it.

Whoever you end up talking to, write down their name and summarize the conversation if anything comes up that differs from the requirements you were given. You'll need this information when you complete the work so that there's a "paper trail" of why this work was done the way it was.

An actual emergency or business priority.

Sometimes, bugs crop up that open security holes or that put the business at immediate risk. This should be *rare* unless you work on an incredibly buggy application or in a truly dysfunctional organization[1]. In any case, you may be faced with a bug that must be fixed as soon as possible, and you or a co-worker know *exactly* what needs to be changed.

What you'll do is to "stop the bleeding" by changing the code that needs changing and push that change to production. Once you've verified that this change fixed the problem, undo the change locally, and start this process from the beginning.

You may get pushback on doing work *after* the "bugfix" has gone up to production, but it would be irresponsible of you to just leave it. You've done first aid only. The symptoms have been addressed, but the underlying problem still needs to be treated.

Unless you are directly ordered to not fix the bug properly, you should get to fixing it using the process described here. Even if you don't "have time", make the time. Your name is now on that line of code and you want it fixed properly.

Pressure to immediately start coding.

A final potential roadblock is that your team lead, co-worker, or project manager might see that you have not immediately started coding and wonder what you are doing. They might feel they've given you everything you need to get started. It's worth taking a second to ask yourself if they are correct. Have you been spending too much time thinking? Use this sort of pushback as a nudge to check yourself.

In most cases it's usually just faster to finish your understanding of the business problem than it is to discuss how long it will take to understand the business problem. My recommendation is to just ignore the comment and finish

---

[1]In that case, you should stop here and read "Landing the Tech Job You Love", referenced in the E

what you are doing. You'll be on your way to delivering good work and the issue will likely be forgotten.

If you can't get away with this, you can simply state that there are a few things you aren't clear on and that you just want to get your bearings before you start. Explain that you only need a few minutes and that you're well on your way to a solution. It's unfortunate to be pushed into making these sorts of promises - you should be trusted to do your job - but this is not always the case.

3.3   Write Tests that Fail

Now that you understand the problem you are solving, your next step is *not* to code the solution, but to write an automated test that intentionally fails, but will succeed when you've solved the problem. Think of this test as an executable "to-do" list. When it passes, you have successfully solved the problem in front of you.

Working test-first is still a controversial topic. Some don't believe in automated tests at all. Others don't see the value in writing them first, while some feel that TDD is "nice to have" but aren't given "permission" to do it. Senior software engineers don't ask permission to do their job. They just do it.

If you are unsure of this approach, or are skeptical that it's the "correct" way to write code, let me try to convince you of both the value of automated tests and the value of writing them first.

The Case for Automated Testing

To know that you have solved the problem in front of you, you will need to execute your code to see if it works (only the most naive and inexperienced developer would ship code that hasn't been executed).

Given this, it's hard to argue that executing your code manually is the right way to do it. Having a script that executes your code is far more efficient. You can press a button to execute your code rather than navigate the user interface.

Having that automated test script packaged as part of your application and runnable by any developer has further advantages. Developers can run such a script to ensure that changes they made haven't introduced bugs into your code. This allows them to code with more confidence. A system could be set up that runs all the automated tests on a regular basis, checking for regressions[2].

Over time your application will develop an automated battery of tests that allow it to be enhanced fearlessly, with each test script indicating where changes in one place have broken another.

This is why we have automated tests. Let's next understand why they should be written before the code they test.

The Case for Writing Tests First

There are two reasons for writing tests first: they encourage you to think about your solution at a code level (not a feature level as we have already done), and, well, writing tests isn't as fun as writing "real" code, so you might as well get it out of the way.

By writing your test first, you are forced to explore the way in which you'd *like* to use your software. It puts you in the role of the user (where *user* might be another developer using your code). Seeing your test fail also indicates that you've successfully transcribed your mental understanding of the problem to code. The test is an executable specification of the problem you need to solve. If you code first, and then write a test that passes, it is **impossible** to know if your code

---

[2]This is typically called "continuous integration" and is an incredibly useful system to have set up.

works, or if your test is bad. Writing the test first is the *easiest* way to be sure of both.

Practically speaking, writing tests isn't as fun as writing "real" code. Test code is ugly, can be hard to read, and is generally not the sort of problem-solving that enamors us with computer programming. But, we've established that having tests is advantageous, bordering on necessary. Given that, why not get it out of the way first?

If writing code is like dessert, writing tests is like eating your vegetables. I can't think of a worse meal than one that started with cake and ended with asparagus.

How to Work Test-First

Although volumes have been written on the subject of test-driven development, I can summarize the main points here as some general guidelines.

We'll assume that your application has an existing test suite and that you can plug into this to start your work (if not, we'll discuss how to deal with it in the Roadblocks section).

What you want to do is to test at the highest level possible to connect your code with your understanding of the problem. For example, suppose you are fixing a bug where certain users get an exception when requesting a certain report. Suppose that the bug is due to the user's font-selection, and the stacktrace of the exception reveals an obvious off-by-one bug in the FontLocator class, which maps the user's chosen font to a file on disk to feed the reporting engine.

You might think that you should add a new unit test to FontLocator as a first step. This would be a mistake. Instead, find the tests for the reporting feature and simulate the bug from the user's perspective by having a test user with a poorly-chosen font generate the report in question.

You must treat the bug as a bug in your *application*, not in any particular unit of code (at least not yet). Remember, your test is an executable encoding of the problem you are solving, and the user's problem is at a much higher level than any function, class, or method.

The same logic applies for implementing small features. You want a test that simulates a user exercising the yet-to-be-implemented feature.

Note that I am not advocating that you *never* write a unit test. You may well end up writing or enhancing some unit tests, but you should always have a test to simulate the problem at hand in the most complete way possible.

Roadblocks

There is no existing test suite.

Despite the popularity of automated tests and the increasingly wide acceptance of writing tests first, you may find yourself in a situation where there is simply no test suite at all. This is a bad situation to be in. You and your team are not well-positioned for success and if you work on projects like this for too long, your career will suffer.

For now, treat this as an opportunity to change things for the better. Hopefully, there are testing frameworks for the technology of your application that can be quickly integrated into your build system. If this is the case, do this setup and configuration and include it in your commit when you're done. Working code will likely win out over any objections from others.

If you don't believe you can do this in a reasonable amount of time, you have two options: work extra hours and "find" the time, or ask permission to take a bit longer so you can set this up. Use your best judgment but in my opinion, asking permission tends to be the most difficult path (we'll talk about making a convincing technical argument in chapter 7).

If you simply cannot get automated tests into your project, you'll need to compromise. Perhaps you can write your test in a shell script or alternate executable. As a last resort, you can simply write out a repeatable process for testing your code and keep it handy. Run your tests periodically and hopefully they'll find a regression, which you can use to bolster your case for automated testing.

On a side note, if you find yourself in this last situation - automated testing is not possible - you need to start finding a new project to work on. This is a red flag and your ability to deliver results and improve as a developer will be seriously hampered.

No infrastructure for tests at the "level" you need to test.

It could be that your application has support for unit tests, but tests at a higher level (such as browser-based or "full stack" acceptance testing) are simply not there.

As in the "no test suite" scenario, I'd recommend you simply add it in yourself. If this is not feasible or possible, you may be able to do a "good enough" job by creating a more complex unit test.

3.4 Solve the Problem as Quickly as You Can

Now that we've eaten our vegetables, it's time for dessert. With your tests failing, you should now get them to pass as expediently as you can. Don't spend a lot of time pondering the "right" solution or making things "elegant". Just get the system working.

Your goal is to make sure that the problem you are solving *can* be solved, and to make sure of this as quickly as possible, without regard to the state of the system when you are done. This allows you to focus completely on making the application work, without being distracted by other concerns such as readability, maintainability, or documentation. We *will* address those issues later, as a separate step.

Many inexperienced (or poor performing) developers will stop here and ship what they've done. This is wrong. It would be as if a real estate developer, having just finished the roof and exterior walls, handed you the keys to the front door. Yes, you have a shelter, but it barely works and would you really want to live there?

With passing tests, you may be tempted to look up from your keyboard at this point and report progress: "I've got it fixed, just need to clean it up". This is also wrong, as it implies something that you cannot be sure of. As we'll see in the next step, we need to address the concerns of maintainability and code cleanliness, and it's not guaranteed that these activities will take less time than you've spent thus far.

Reporting progress here is making a promise you can't necessarily keep and is the perfect example of why you should keep the details of how you deliver results private. Yes, you're using a technique to organize your work and, by getting your tests to pass, you *have* made progress. But, you aren't done and you don't know precisely *when* you'll be done. This means you don't actually have anything useful to report. Your work is still "in progress".

Roadblocks

This part of the process is unlikely to encounter pushback because it appears to outsiders that you are doing what is thought of as "programming": typing feverishly into the computer.

If you do any pair programming, your pair might take issue with your tactic of coding without regard to cleanliness, style, or maintainability. Simply remind your pair that once things are working, you can use the test suite to keep things working while you clean everything up. Since this is such a small bugfix or feature, you can only make so much of a mess.

3.5 Modify Your Code for Maintainability and Readability

In the classic "TDD Cycle", the third step is "Refactor". Like testing, refactoring is a huge topic and there are many techniques that can be applied. These specific techniques are well covered in other books, so let's instead talk about the general idea and purpose of this step.

In the previous step, you solved the problem as quickly as possible and now have something that works but that may lack *cleanliness*. You focused on making the system pass its test, but you weren't thinking about the maintainability or comprehensibility of the code. It's likely your solution is a bit sloppy and should be improved.

Even the smallest change has room for improvement, and it's always a good idea to review your work looking for things to clean up. In the end, you want the codebase to be easy to understand and easy to modify.

Start by looking at the diff of your changes. This diff represents the change you are making to the system. You want this change to be the *smallest possible change*. "Small" doesn't necessarily mean lines of code. It could also mean the easiest thing to understand or fewest number of additional concepts.

Ideally, another developer can look at your diff and know exactly what you did and what effect that will have on the system. At a superficial level, this means:

No copy and paste code Duplication is a bug waiting to happen.

Descriptive variable names The names you used initially might make sense to you, but do they make sense when you look at the code as a whole? Rename liberally, and don't be afraid to use long, descriptive names if needed.

Coding style should match the code in the file You aren't solving the problem of where parenthesis, semicolons, or braces go. Write your code the way the previous author did, even if it's not your preferred style. It makes understanding the diff a *lot* easier for everyone.

There are *many* ways to clean the code up beyond these simple steps. There are many common "smell tests" you could perform to draw your attention to areas that might need to change. Perhaps your change added sufficient lines of code to a method that it is now "too long". Perhaps you added code to a class that is now doing "too many things".

Code smells (like the ones listed here), are a good way to objectively evaluate your change for understandability and maintainability.

Make changes one at a time, re-running your tests after each change. This way, if a test should fail, you know what change you made that caused it.

A Word on Code Comments

When you are looking for code that might need improvement, *any* time you see a comment, that is a place to consider refactoring (especially if it's a comment you wrote during the previous step). In many cases, you can eliminate the need for comments by making the code better or more clear.

Consider this contrived method, written in Ruby:

```
# Updates the persons rendering settings.
```

27

```
# person:: The Person to update
# settings:: A RenderingSettings instance
def update_person(person,settings)
  # ..
end
```

It's nice that an attempt was made to document the API, but this code would be a lot clearer if we combined the comments with the method and variable names, like so:

```
def update_person_rendering_settings(
    person,rendering_settings)
  # ..
end
```

Now the method says what it does and the variable names follow a common Ruby idiom of being named like their type (i.e. we can assume that a variable rendering_settings, if undocumented, is an instance of RenderingSettings)

Be careful not to treat all comments as bad. Comment-free code can be difficult to understand, as it often lacks the context or "why" of the code.

This is often the case if you must implement something based on strange requirements or with an odd API that results in code that looks buggy, but really isn't.

For example, suppose we have the concept of a "primary" report and a series of "secondary" reports, and we are writing a feature to render only the "secondary" reports. Suppose further that the reporting system exposes reports in an array with the first one being considered "primary".

This design is not ideal, but the problem we need to solve *isn't* to improve the reporting systems design. We simply need to work with it to add a new feature (it might not even be possible to fix this design flaw if you don't have access to the source code).

We might end up with code like this (if you aren't familiar with Java, see appendix D.2 for an *incredibly* brief overview):

```java
public void renderSecondaryReports(
    List<Report> reports) {
  for(int i=1; i<reports.size(); i++) {
    renderReport(reports.get(i));
  }
}
```

Most programmers will see the int i=1 and immediately suspect this is an off-by-one error, since most programming languages use 0 as the first index into a collection. If another developer doesn't know about the convention of storing "secondary" reports at index 1, they might "fix" the problem by changing the starting index to 0.

Although someone could piece this together by looking at the tests (assuming they exist and cover this case), it would save everyone a lot of time and head-scratching to just add a comment here:

```java
public void renderSecondaryReports(
    List<Report> reports) {
  // recall that reports[0] is the primary report,
  // so we skip it
  for(int i=1; i<reports.size(); i++) {
    renderReport(reports.get(i));
  }
}
```

This should be a rare case, but illustrates the difference between delivering the right solution and wasting time over-engineering. Your job isn't to "fix" the reporting system's data model.

Finally, you might find that it takes longer to make code clearer than it did to write it in the first place. This is neither unusual nor an indicator that anything is wrong. Part of the reason you should resist reporting progress before starting this step is to give yourself the freedom to refactor what's needed instead of what you have "time for".

Don't Over-Engineer and Know When to Quit

It can occasionally be hard to know when you are "done". The existence of tests can be so freeing that you may find yourself tweaking and perfecting your code past the point where it's worth it. Or, you may be tempted to start refactoring code unrelated to the change at hand just to "clean things up". This can work against you and make the system, and your change, harder to understand.

To deal with this, you must adopt the mindset that clean code is not the same as "elegant" or "perfect" code. Many developers consider code either "100% sloppy" or "100% elegant". It's really more of a continuum, with "clean" being somewhere in between.

The example above regarding the "secondary" reports concept perfectly illustrates this. You might be tempted to try to correct the poor design of storing reports in an array where the first is the "primary" one by convention. This would be over-engineering, because such a change would not only be outside the scope of what you're doing, but also be much more drastic.

A rule of thumb is to restrict your activities to *refactoring*, using the most literal definition of the word:

> [Refactoring is] restructuring an existing body of code, altering its internal structure without changing its external behavior

In your case, the "external behavior" should be at the lowest possible level, for example a method signature. If, after getting your feature to work, or fixing your bug, you feel that you need to change method signature, class names, or other code that will ripple outside your change, you might be over-engineering.

This isn't to say that re-designing poorly-developed code is bad, or that you should never undertake a serious change to the system (we'll talk about that in chapter 4). It's just that the task in front of you - the results you are asked to deliver - should be done as expediently as possible allowing for a clean and maintainable solution. Redesigns of parts of the system should be done later, as a separate task.

The result of fixing a bug or implementing a small feature is different than the result of cleaning up code that's hard to work with. Being honest and explicit about this difference will help you deliver results quickly and consistently, as well as keep you focused.

Make your solution clean, but make the smallest change you can. Once you've done this, it's time to commit your changes and share your solution with the team.

Roadblocks

Like the previous step, this step "looks" like what anyone expects programmers to do: staring at the screen and typing. When pair-programming, this step might result in more discussion. This can be a good thing since if two programmers can agree that a particular refactoring is good, chances are it is.

3.6 Commit Your Changes

Now that you've verified that your code solves the problem you were given, and your solution is clean and maintainable, it's time to get your changes incorporated into the source code of the application. Hopefully, your team has some sort of process for this, such as submitting a patch, issuing a pull request, or simply committing the code to source control.

Whatever the mechanism, you'll need to come up with some sort of commit message to go along with your change. Many developers will gloss over this step and write a terse or vague message. Instead, you should take special care to write a good message. Other than clean code, this is one of the most important steps in the process.

Think of a commit message as a special kind of code comment. Your commit represents a snapshot of the code at the time you changed it and your message is the note on the back of that snapshot. Your message will persist even after the code you've just changed is changed again.

A developer (possibly yourself) looking at the code in the future might have questions about the way it's written and the commit message is one place a developer will look. You want that developer to get answers from your commit message.

The first line of your commit message should state, as briefly and specifically as possible, what the change is. "Fixed bug" or "Updated config" are brief, but not specific. "Fixed bug in FontRenderer" is better and "Fixed bug where FontRenderer blows up on non-existent font" is fantastic.

The remainder of your commit message should detail anything else about the commit, such as:

- A link to your trouble-ticket system or project management tool for this change. This allows other developers to find all the details about this change, if needed.

- Details about conversations you had (and with whom) about this change. If you were unable to talk directly to the stakeholder, this is where you'd transcribe your notes about who you talked to and what was decided regarding this change, e.g. "Jim mentioned we should skip zeros, even though the requirements themselves were vague. We couldn't find Larry to clarify". Don't think of this as placing blame, but as simply recording notes in a permanent, searchable fashion.

- Explanations as to why you did things a certain way, especially if the diff itself might have some oddities to it.

Do *not* explain the code itself. Assume that person reading this message has read and understood the diff and can see how the code actually works.

Once you've done this, you've now made a simple, clean change to the system that delivers the exact value required, as quickly as was reasonably possible, and everything is documented and comprehensible by other developers.

Now that we understand these basic five steps, let's see how it works in practice.

3.7 Example

Suppose you work on the reporting end of an e-commerce system that shows, among other things, a report of money spent per hour in a graph. Administrators of your company use this graph to look for trends in purchasing.

You receive the following bug report:

The purchasing graph is not rendering trends accurately. Certain outlying data points are causing the graph to look erratic. We'd like to smooth it out by omitting readings less than $10 and greater than $100,000.

Seems straightforward enough, but it's not clear *why* this needs to be done. Why would we omit readings outside of a range? Wouldn't that make the graph less accurate?

Understand the Problem

You first ask the project manager, Ronnie, for more information.

"Hmm, I'm not sure actually. Why do you need to know?"

You respond: "I know it's a minor change, but just in case there are other issues, knowing why we're doing something that, to me, seems to reduce the accuracy of the graph, will really help make sure I do the right thing"

"Good point", Ronnie says. "I got this from Curtis, the purchasing admin lead, let's go ask him."

You head over to Curtis' desk and ask.

"Oh yeah," Curtis starts, "we were seeing some really strange data on those graphs, and it turned out that there is a bug in the data import that sometimes includes very small or very large values that are correct in aggregate, but that mess up our analysis. Since we get that data from Wilshire, there's not much we can about it but filter it out."

"Wouldn't it be be easier to have the data import team filter these out?" you ask.

Curtis replies: "No, because we aren't the only ones using that data. I think that Gilroy's team actually needs to see the values we want filtered. For us, we use that graph for trends and predictions, and the outliers make that difficult. We don't need *exact* data on those graphs, so we figured this was a data visualization concern."

Curtis is right, you thank him for his time, and go back to your desk. Ronnie updates the feature description in your feature management tool with this background info.

Write Tests That Fail

The graph data is generated by a class called `PurchasingGraphFilter` that takes raw input data and returns "graph-able" data for the user interface. The existing implementation simply strips nulls and negative values:

```java
public class PurchasingGraphFilter {
  public List<DataPoint> filter(
      Collection<DataPoint> points) {

    List<DataPoint> filtered = new ArrayList<DataPoint>();
    for (DataPoint dataPoint: points) {
      if ((dataPoint != null) &&
        (dataPoint.value() >= 0)) {
        filtered.add(dataPoint);
      }
    }
    return filtered;
  }
}
```

The tests cover this pretty well and, luckily, all the values in the tests are between 11 and 99,999. This means they should still pass once you've made your changes (if this were not the case, you'd need to change those tests as well).

Testing the new feature can be done with one test. You create a list of data points that has a mixture of values below 10, above 100,000, and in between. When you're done coding, the call to `filter` should not include the values below 10 or above 100,000.

```java
public PurchasingGraphFilterText extends TestCase {
  // ... existing test methods ...

  @Test
```

```
public void testStrippingOutliers {
  List<DataPoint> points = Arrays.asList(
    new DataPoint(9),      // filtered
    new DataPoint(10),     // filtered
    new DataPoint(11),     // not filtered
    new DataPoint(99999),  // not filtered
    new DataPoint(100000),// filtered
    new DataPoint(100001) // filtered
  );
  List<DataPoint> filtered =
    new PurchasingGraphFilter().filter(points);

  assertEquals(2,filtered.size(),
      filtered.toString());
  assertEquals(11,filtered.get(0).value());
  assertEquals(99999,filtered.get(1).value());
  }
}
```

You've smartly tested along the boundaries of the relevant filter values (e.g. that 10 is filtered, but 11 is not).

Running the test, you see it fail precisely as designed: the filtered list has more elements than expected. Since you included the contents of the filtered list in your test failure message, you can easily observe that the values 9, 10, 100,000, and 100,001 are still included in the list after filtering. Now, you set your mind to getting this test passing.

Get Tests to Pass

Flipping back to the main source, you start writing code to get the test passing. It's simple enough to add new conditions to the existing if statement, so you do just that:

```
public class PurchasingGraphFilter {
  public List<DataPoint> filter(
```

```
      Collection<DataPoint> points) {
    List<DataPoint> filtered =
        new ArrayList<DataPoint>();
      for (DataPoint dataPoint: points) {
        if ((dataPoint != null)        &&
            (dataPoint.value() >= 0) &&
            (dataPoint.value() > 10) &&
            (dataPoint.value() < 100000) {
          filtered.add(dataPoint);
        }
      }
    return dataPoint;
  }
}
```

Running the tests, you see them all pass. You've gotten the new feature working, and haven't broken anything in the process.

The solution isn't elegant - it's quite ugly in fact - but it validates that this feature can be added and made to work.

This is only a "first draft", so the messiness is OK. Next, you want to clean this up, letting your tests ensure that your code continues to work.

Refactor

You take a moment and re-read your code. Three things jump out as being a bit messy:

- You've hard-coded the "magic" values 10 and 100,000.

- The if statement's expression is very complex.

- There's a duplicate condition as well: if a value is greater than 10, it is also greater than or equal to 0.

37

You decide that replacing the magic values with constants and then extracting the if statement's expression to a method will make the code clearer.

```
public class PurchasingGraphFilter {
  public List<DataPoint> filter(
      Collection<DataPoint> points) {
    List<DataPoint> filtered =
      new ArrayList<DataPoint>();
    for (DataPoint dataPoint: points) {
      if ((dataPoint != null) &&
          inAllowableRange(dataPoint)) {
        filtered.add(dataPoint);
      }
    }
    return dataPoint;
  }

  private static final int OUTLIER_MIN = 10;
  private static final int OUTLIER_MAX = 100000;

  private boolean inAllowableRange(
      DataPoint dataPoint) {
    return (dataPoint.value() > OUTLIER_MIN) &&
        (dataPoint.value() < OUTLIER_MAX);
  }
}
```

You re-run the tests and they continue to pass; the refactoring was good. Now, when you re-read the code, it's a lot more clear. The public method filter is concise and readable, and the extracted method inAllowableRange is also a lot simpler than the if expression it was extracted from. The addition of the constants OUTLIER_MIN and OUTLIER_MAX also make the expression easier to understand as well as encode that these values are specifically outliers (as opposed to some other range-based constraint).

This code is now clean, maintainable, and ready to ship. Let's take a brief detour and continue refactoring - past when we should - to see what an over-engineered solution looks like.

Over-Engineering

You start to realize that this class would be more flexible if the outliers weren't constants, but members of the class, configurable via the constructor. You continue refactoring to the following:

```java
public class PurchasingGraphFilter {

  private final int outlierMin;
  private final int outlierMax;

  public PurchasingGraphFilter() {
    this(10,100000);
  }

  public PurchaseGraphFilter(int outlierMin,
                             int outlierMax) {
    this.outlierMin = outlierMin;
    this.outlierMax = outlierMax;
  }

  public List<DataPoint> filter(
      Collection<DataPoint> points) {
    List<DataPoint> filtered =
      new ArrayList<DataPoint>();
    for (DataPoint dataPoint: points) {
      if ((dataPoint != null) &&
          inAllowableRange(dataPoint)) {
        filtered.add(dataPoint);
      }
    }
```

```
    return filtered;
  }

  private boolean inAllowableRange(
      DataPoint dataPoint) {
    return (dataPoint.value() > this.outlierMax) &&
           (dataPoint.value() < this.outlierMax);
  }
}
```

We've now created two constructors: one that accepts any values for the outliers, and one that defaults them to the values from our original requirements. The class is backwards-compatible, but also more flexible. By creating two constructors, one that accepts any outliers and a second that Flexibility is good, right?

Not always. In this case, it's made the code worse:

- You have no requirement to change the min and max values and, if you did get one later, it would be simple enough to add that configureability at that time. Adding it now isn't buying us anything.

- There's more code to maintain.

- The class is conceptually more complex. Someone trying to understand its role in the system now has to look for *two* ways of constructing it: the default, and the configurable.

- You'll need to add tests for the new constructor.

- The flexibility now contains a bug. You forgot to check that outlierMin is actually less than outlierMax in the constructor.

- It's possible that a future feature will actually require a custom constructor for other reasons and we've made *that* job harder to do.

Basically, you've misunderstood what it means to make the system easy to change and maintainable. Although the class itself is more flexible, there's no need for that flexibility, and the overall system is *harder* to change and *harder* to understand because of it.

Realizing this, you undo your last refactoring and prepare to ship the right solution. Although this solution was purposefully over-engineered, it's important to understand that undoing mistakes and backing off from an approach that isn't working out is always an option. Save the code in a private branch or personal notebook if you want to refer to it, but always eliminate it if it's not working.

Committing your Change

You've added your test, gotten it working, and cleaned it up. Now, you tailor your commit message:

```
Make purchase graph easier to interpret

Per Curtis, the purchasing admins do not need to
see values that are "too low" or "too high",
even though, in aggregate, those values are valid.
So, we just filter them out.

See http://bugtracker.example.com/features/4567
```

You've perfectly summarized what the change was and why it was made as well as where to find more information. Your team lead accepts the changes and pushes it to production.

3.8   Is This Much Process Really Necessary?

If you have never worked this way, the process may feel "heavy" and time consuming. You might feel like you are just fine banging out code and checking it manually, at least for such small things.

The reality is, this process requires more details and time to describe than to follow. Anytime you write code, you're going to have to understand what you need to do, write the code to do it, check that it works, and submit your changes to the main codebase.

All we're doing here is providing a simple and repeatable process that results in high quality work, delivered in a short amount of time. I'm not just making this up out of thin air. As mentioned, this is based on TDD, which is widely used in the industry.

Finally, if you are still skeptical, I would highly advise you try this for a few features or bugfixes and see how it feels. I was skeptical for many years about writing tests first, but once I started doing it, I didn't want to stop. I find working this way to be incredibly freeing and feel I write better code because of it, especially for the sorts of small things we're talking about here.

3.9   Moving On

This covers a personal process for small enhancements and bugfixes. This is the foundation for all of the code-related techniques that we'll discuss.

An important thing to note about this process is that it's *personal*. No matter what job you have or what task you have in front of you, you can structure your work this way without "permission" or without even telling anyone that you're working this way. Think of yourself as a class with the public method `implementSmallFeature()` but whose implementation is private.

As you start working this way, the quality of your work will go up, as will your understanding of the systems on which you work. Because you've taken the time to understand the problem, both at a human and a code level and because you've organized your time around making sure your solution is the right one, you can be sure that you've done the right thing, and done it properly. You'll be focused on delivering results like never before.

For more complex coding challenges, such as large features or entirely new applications, this technique won't be entirely sufficient. We'll need to use this technique as part of a larger process, which we'll see in the next chapter.

4

Add Features with Ease

The personal process we outlined in the previous chapter will serve you well for most simple programming tasks, such as bugfixes and small features. For larger tasks, however, you'll need to make a few adjustments and additions to your process.

In this chapter, we'll talk about implementing features that are larger than a simple bugfix, but not large enough to require coordinated effort among many developers. Basically, we're talking about features that one developer (or one pair) can do in a few days or weeks.

While you could just use the process we outlined in the previous chapter - many developers do - this isn't ideal for tasks at this level of complexity. That process is entirely designed to produce code in small, focused bursts. You'll do that here, but iteratively, as part of a coordinated effort to change the codebase. This coordination requires some up-front knowledge and planning (for lack of a better term; we won't be creating UML diagrams, I promise).

The basic process, as outlined in figure 4.1, is:

1. Understand the problem

2. Understand the system

3. Create acceptance-level tests for the feature

4. Plan your implementation

5. Repeat the cycle from the previous chapter until all your acceptance-level tests pass

6. Get a code review

7. Commit your changes

Don't be afraid of the number of steps. As with our bugfix process, this is mostly codifying what you are likely already doing by adding some structure and a bit more formality. You'll notice that we've basically wrapped the process from the previous chapter with some additional steps. These steps are here to deal with the complexity of the change you'll be making.

4.1   Understand the Problem

Your job here is identical to that in the previous chapter, but it is more important, since the change you are making is more significant. You should push hard to meet with a user or project stakeholder to talk through the feature.

Before you meet, become intimately familiar with the documentation you've been given, and make sure you have a solid understanding of the features related to this new feature.

If you've been given a user interface (UI) mockup, familiarize yourself with that, possibly even clarifying things with the designer, and bring it to the meeting.

Figure 4.1: Basic Workflow for Implementing a Feature

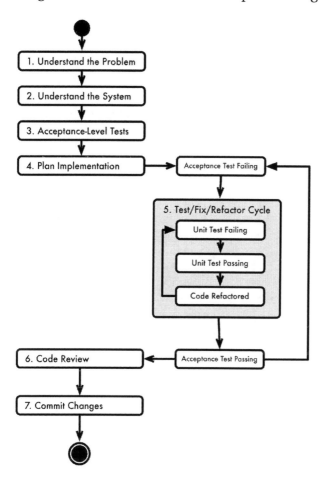

If you have not been given a UI mockup or are expected to produce the UI on your own, schedule two meetings with your user/stakeholder: one to talk through the business problem, and a second to talk through the UI. If you are new to creating UI mockups, just keep it simple. Often a drawing on a piece of paper is sufficient to work out how something should look, but there are many web-based and desktop tools to create UI mockups.

Any new information that comes out of this meeting should be documented and emailed back to the stakeholder. This serves as a "checksum" that you both took away the same thing from the meeting.

This may sound more formal than what we talked about in the last chapter, and to a certain extent it is, but it's still not something that requires hours of preparation or the attendance of a flock of managers. Your meeting will still be an informal chat at your desk (or the stakholder's). You could even do this over chat or instant messenger.

The meeting plus your prep time shouldn't take more than an hour unless your specification is very poor or the feature is quite complex (in which case the time spent understanding the problem now is even more crucial).

Remember, your goal is to fully understand what should be delivered and, more importantly, why. Without that information, you have a high chance of doing the wrong thing or implementing the feature in a less-than-ideal way (both of which will result in expensive rework later).

Roadblocks

Stakeholder is not available/accessible.

As with our personal process for bugfixes, it's possible that the project stakeholders or users are inaccessible to you, and that you just won't be able to meet with them to get an understanding of the business problem. It's more important here that you *do* meet with them, so you might push a bit harder than you otherwise would to see if it's possible.

If you are unable to meet with them, find a proxy, such as your project manager or team lead. In this case however, you should change the way you ultimately solve the problem. Since you haven't talked to the person who will ultimately use (or who requested) what you are building, take a more conservative approach in your design. You should strive to make your change as small as you absolutely can, since this is the best way to account for changes later due to changing or clarified requirements.

4.2 Understand the System

Now that you understand the business problem you are solving and the way in which the user will interact with the system to do so, you need to develop a *system view* of the application you'll need to modify.

Developing a system view is part of *systems thinking*, which Wikipedia defines as follows:

> ...an approach to problem solving, by viewing "problems" as parts of an overall system, rather than reacting to specific parts, outcomes, or events and potentially contributing to further development of unintended consequences.

The key is the phrase "unintended consequences". Because the change you're making is complex, there is a risk of inadvertently breaking a seemingly unrelated part of the system by implementing your feature incorrectly.

Depending on the size of the system you're working with, it might not be feasible to develop a deep system view of the entire application. You should get the broadest view you can in the context of your change. Answering these questions will help:

- What domain objects will this feature need to interact with?

- What business rules exist around those objects?

- What structures are in place to manage those objects?

- What new objects will you need to create?

- What is the test coverage like? Will you need to add test coverage anywhere before making changes?

- Are there any offline tasks related to these objects?

- Is there special reporting or auditing on the changes related to these objects, and should your new objects be a part of this?

- Are there non-functional requirements to consider, such as performance or security?

Depending on your familiarity with the system and the complexity of the feature, you may need to document some of this. I'm not advocating a formal design document, but drawing process flows and other visual aides on a whiteboard or piece of paper can make it much simpler to understand how a piece of code or system works.

Further, writing down an explanation of something you think you understand is a good way to ensure you actually understand it. Often, when reverse-engineering a design from code, you'll find edge cases or other avenues to explore. You might even find a few bugs.

Keep in mind that whatever you produce here is *not a work product*. It's intermediate work to help you understand the system you're modifying. Treat it as private and disposable (although I've found that such documents and diagrams are useful far longer than I thought, as they help to "re-gain" a system view of parts of the application I haven't touched in a while; consider keeping these in a private folder or putting up in a shared wiki as reference).

Roadblocks

Pressure to immediately start coding.

Your team lead or co-workers may observe you reading code, writing down things, and drawing on whiteboards. Hopefully, the degree to which you are conspicuously documenting the system is inversely proportional to your understanding of it and that this can serve as the explanation.

It can also be helpful to engage your lead or co-workers who are asking about what you are doing. This can speed things along and turn a potentially adversarial question into a helpful collaboration session.

4.3 Create Acceptance-Level Tests

At this point, you understand the problem being solved, and have a solid understanding of the system you'll be working with. Before you start work, you need to create an acceptance-level test of the feature you are building.

An *acceptance test* simulates a user using the feature as closely as possible (i.e. the user is "accepting" that the feature works as desired). For example, in a web-based application, your acceptance tests might launch a web browser that exercises parts of the application.

When you start coding, your focus will change from the high-level view you have now to a lower-level view of the code. The acceptance tests can let you quickly figure out where you are when you put your head up from the code. Think of them as an executable "todo" list.

Writing acceptance tests is its own book, but hopefully your system has some written already that you can use as a reference for how to add yours. Your main goal is to test that the features outlined in the requirements you were given are all working as intended. You don't need to cover every esoteric edge case (although you should certainly exercise some), but you want all the "happy paths" to be covered end-to-end.

51

Roadblocks

No acceptance-level tests exist in the system.

When dealing with this problem for smaller bugfixes where there were no tests, I recommended that you simply add tests and the test framework as part of your final commit. I'd still recommend that here, especially given the increased risk in not testing a larger change to the system.

Further, since your overall task is going to take a longer time, the addition of acceptance-level testing support to the application will be a smaller percentage of the time you spend on the task as a whole, making it more worthwhile.

If you absolutely cannot automate these tests in any reasonable way, I would recommend writing out manual test scripts. Remember that your goal is to encode your knowledge of the problem and what "done" means. Ideally, that's in code, but if it can't be, encode it as a series of steps that you will manually follow before calling your work "done".

Perception that acceptance tests are the job of QA.

Many organizations leave testing at this level to a dedicated QA team. If you get pushback on creating acceptance tests before coding or are told that QA must be involved, request that a member of the QA team be assigned now, while you have the best understanding of the problem. The longer you wait to involve QA, the more poorly they will perform, because they'll lack the information to completely test the feature.

If this isn't possible, you have two choices: you can create the tests anyway, ignoring questions (or hiding what you are doing), or you can create manual tests scripts as described above and hope for the best.

This is a particularly toxic type of roadblock, because it's in direct conflict with you producing your best work and delivering the most value. It will also increase the burden of testing later as you won't have any high-level executable tests.

4.4 Plan your Implementation

The word "plan" might set off some alarm bells in your head, especially if you subscribe to agile methodologies which promote the notion of "No Big Design Up Front". Even without a particularly strong viewpoint on "agile", you might be tempted to just start coding.

Given that this feature is more complex than a bugfix, it means that there are many ways to go about it, and the best way might not become apparent just from coding.

If you take a moment to imagine the system with the new feature implemented, you can quickly cut off avenues of development that won't work out. By plotting out your work before starting, you'll also be more likely to re-use existing code in the system, and produce a cleaner solution.

You aren't looking to generate some detailed publishable documentation. In fact, your "plan" might be developed entirely in your head. The point is to think a bit about how you're going to get this task done and create a mental roadmap of how it will work.

Exactly *how* to go about this is highly dependent on your work style. Some developers like to-do lists, others like to put comments in the code where they need to make changes, while others will draw before/after system flow diagrams.

Do whatever you need to visualize and understand the steps you'll take. If you cannot explain to another developer how you're going to solve this problem or what the state of the system will be after you're done, you are ill-equipped to start coding.

The best approach to getting a solid plan in place is to actually do that: discuss it with another developer. Find your nearest co-worker (or technical lead) and talk them through your approach. This can save quite a bit of time since any errors in your approach won't otherwise get caught until code review, where the cost of change is higher.

Whatever you do, *resist the urge to publicize your plan.* This plan is not a result you are delivering and doing so is a promise you can't (or shouldn't) keep. Certain types of project managers would love to see something like this, so they could check off the tasks and derive some sort of "percent complete" for your feature. This is dangerous for two reasons:

- These tasks aren't the same amount of effort - it could be that most of your time is taken up by one or two of these tasks

- As you work, you will learn more about the system and the change you are making, which may change these plans. You may not need or want to update your todo list instead "riding the wave" of changes you encounter. Being beholden to others to follow your to-do list (or keep it up to date) is a distraction that takes your focus away from delivering results.

Whatever you produce here is for your internal use only and is designed to capture your thinking at a high level about how to solve the problem and what bases need covering. Once you dive into the code, you will focus on much smaller concerns. Your "plan" here is for those moments when you get done with something and stick your head up to see where you are.

This is different from your acceptance tests because those tests deal with features of the application and the user's view. Your plan here is about the code you'll need to change.

Roadblocks

Pressure to immediately start coding.

Hopefully, your planning will be internal and not exposed to your tech lead or project manager. If they *do* see what you're doing and feel that you should "just start coding", I would recommend you ignore them to the extent possible.

If you are forced to address their concern, simply explain that you are getting organized before you start coding and, if they will allow you to get back to it, you'll be coding soon. Extreme micro-management will prevent you from delivering results and you should discourage it whenever possible.

Unable to create a plan or mental model AKA "Coders Block".

You may find that you have no idea where to start and are not sure what steps you need to take. The complexity of the task (especially if you are inexperienced) can be overwhelming.

It could be that your systems view isn't sufficient and that you need to take more time reading through the code to know where to start. If you feel you have a good understanding of the system, try starting with the entry point or user interface.

If this doesn't help, a technique I've found useful is to make what I call a "sketch". To make a sketch, simply start making disposable changes to the code that implement the feature. Go quickly, ignoring edge cases, tests, and cleanliness. As you sketch the solution, you'll develop a better understanding of where in the code you need to make changes, and what those changes might be.

Once you get to a stopping point, get a diff of your changes. This diff should help you form your plan of attack. Once you've got this, undo all of these changes and start fresh with the test-driven process. Saving the diff for reference might be useful (e.g. in a private branch in your version control system), but you don't want to actually use any code written this way.

4.5 Repeat the Test/Fix/Refactor Cycle

Now, you're ready to start writing some code. What you want to do here is follow your plan and write the code you need by writing tests that fail, writing code to make those tests pass, and then refactoring what you've done.

Your goal here is to repeat this cycle frequently, which could be several times an hour or more. You want your tests passing as frequently as possible, and you want to take small steps in your implementation, stopping regularly to refactor (as opposed to writing a huge suite of tests first, getting them all to pass, and then performing a massive refactoring).

Work in Small Steps

The advantage to working in such small steps is that when you inevitably realize something you missed, or when you go down the wrong path, you'll know it quickly. You can either reverse course or make whatever changes to your plan you need, knowing that you've spent the least amount of time possible working on the wrong thing.

Update your plan only as necessary. Often, the plan itself is disposable; merely creating it is sufficient. Your plan's value was in getting started but, if you feel that updating it as you learn more about what you need to do is helpful, by all means do so. Just don't treat it as a work product that must reflect how you actually implemented this change.

At the end of each step, make sure to refactor and clean up what you've done, as it can save a lot of time later on. I call this "working clean".

Work Clean

My wife and I once hosted a dinner party and, while preparing the main course, we realized that the kitchen was in such disarray that we couldn't serve any more food without cleaning part of the kitchen.

Compare this to a professional kitchen, where the chefs produce *far* more food for *far* more people, *far* more quickly. These kitchens are almost always perfectly clean, even if there are several dishes being prepared at once. Each new dish is prepared from a clean kitchen, no matter what time of day or night it is. This is because the chefs clean as they go, never letting the mess build up.

This is what you want to strive for when you code. Once you have passing tests, you should stop and refactor. This might be as simple as renaming a variable to make it more clear, extracting complex logic into a private method, or even creating entirely new classes that simplify what you've done.

As you produce more and more changes, the refactorings that might be needed could become larger and larger. Don't be afraid to make those refactorings and always do so in the context of your *entire* change, not just the changes you've made in your current "test/fix" cycle.

Just as it's easier to prepare food in a clean kitchen, it's easier to write new code in a clean codebase. If you need to clean up something to continue working, so be it, but also keep *your* work clean as well.

Roadblocks

Overwhelmed with complexity.

It may be hard to go from your plan to taking small steps and following the test/fix/refactor cycle we've talked about. This is the complexity of software design. Volumes have been written on the subject, and there's no chance we can do them justice here, but the key to managing complexity is to be organized, take things one step at a time, and not to be afraid to undo things that end up being bad decisions.

As developers, we have it very easy in this regard. The only cost to change is time. If you make a mistake or go down the wrong path, all you need to do is undo your work and start over. You haven't wasted any raw materials, so just take a breath and go again.

I would recommend you take breaks frequently, away from the computer. Go for a walk, grab a cup of tea, or talk with a co-worker about something unrelated to your project. This will allow your brain some rest and you'll find that you can approach your next problem much more easily.

When you're coding, don't be afraid to take the "long way" if it means you can work in small steps. For example, you might realize you need to change the public interface of a widely-used class to get your work done, so that you can re-use that class's business logic without duplicating code.

This could be a large change, so you might take a small step of copying the code you need to re-use to a new class, leaving the original alone. In a later step, you can unify the two classes to remove the copy and paste, once you have your end of things working.

The beauty of the test/fix/refactor cycle is that your tests allow you to write horrible hacky things to just "get it working", because you know that you will clean it all up later. Not every line of code you write now will be in your final commit, so don't stress about it.

4.6   Get a Code Review

Since the change you are making here is larger than the sorts of changes we talked about in the previous chapter, it's important to get someone else to look over what you've done. Even if you are practicing pair programming, you should still try to get someone unfamiliar with the problem to see if your solution makes sense.

If your team or organization doesn't have a culture of code reviews, you will need to guide the reviewer through the process. Even if your team does regular code reviews, you still want to help the reviewer(s) as much as possible.

Preparing the Review

Your request for a code review should have two parts: guidance from you and the diff of your changes. Tools like Github make this very simple, as you can submit a pull request, and provide review guidance there.

Your guidance should help the reviewer know where to start. Although you are intimately familiar with this set of changes, remember that the reviewer is coming in cold.

First, you want to summarize what the feature is and what problem it solves in just a few short sentences. You should also provide a link to the detailed requirements for reference, but it's important to summarize things right in the review so the reviewer doesn't have to go hunting down a longer document.

If your solution is complex, you might spend a few sentences summarizing your general approach, so the reviewer understands your thinking. Next, you should list, in order, the classes/files that the reviewer should read to understand the change. If you aren't sure how to do this, just start with the UI portion, and trace things down to the back-end. The idea is to guide the reviewer so you get good feedback and not questions about where things are.

If there are specific types of feedback you want, ask for them. For example, you might be nervous about a change related to security, and could ask the reviewer to pay close attention to that. This will help the reviewer focus on what's most important to you, if they are unable to completely review your changes.

The diff you provide should be in a form to allow the reviewer to see both the proposed changes (a diff) as well as the entire state of the codebase that includes your changes. Most modern version control systems have a facility for doing this.

Responding to Feedback

As the review proceeds, you'll hopefully get a lot of feedback. It's important that you understand and respond appropriately to the feedback you receive. This is not only to improve the correctness of your solution, but also to let the reviewer know that their time has not been wasted.

The type of feedback you'll get will fall roughly into one of three categories:

Code is wrong Code can be "wrong" for a few reasons. Most obviously, it could contain a bug. More subtly, it could go against the application's architecture or the team's coding conventions (e.g. a convention around never putting raw SQL into a web view template). Finally, it could be done in a bad way due to ignorance of the codebase. For example, you may have re-implemented something that already exists elsewhere in the code.

Hopefully you won't get comments about your code being "wrong", but this sort of feedback is the most important function of a code review. If the reviewer is correct that a particular piece of code is wrong, simply respond with "good catch, will fix", and make the required change.

If the code is actually correct, but the reviewer mis-interpreted it, then their comment is really a case of "the code is confusing".

Code is confusing This feedback can come in a variety of forms, but basically it comes down to the reviewer not understanding what you've written. No matter how clear you think it is, the fact that it's not clear to the reviewer essentially means the code is unclear.

Often, a reviewer will suggest a way to make it more clear. Although their suggestion might be a good one, feel free to ignore it, and respond with whatever you think would be an improvement. The message that the code is confusing is more important than the suggestion about how to correct it.

To fix this, treat it as a refactoring. Improve the code for clarity using your tests to make sure you haven't broken anything.

Style/aesthetic issue If your team or company has a "house style", and the reviewer has pointed out a deviation, you should simply correct the code to match the house style. Regardless of your feelings on the existing coding style conventions, your responsibility is to follow them. Changing them is something you should take up with the team later, not as part of your current task.

If on the other hand, the reviewer's stylistic comment isn't related to an existing coding convention, and you disagree with their suggestion, you'll need to decide who "wins".

If you will be maintaining and working with this code for the foreseeable future, your style should be favored. If the reviewer will be maintaining this code, however, you should favor their style, as long as it doesn't affect correctness or readability. The person most responsible for the code should be given the final say on aesthetic issues.

One final note about dealing with feedback is if the conversation starts to go in circles, or there is a lot of back-and-forth discussion, it might be worth having a face-to-face chat about the more hotly contested issues. While asynchronous reviews are very efficient with everyone's time (as well as great at providing a paper trail), it's possible to reach an impasse that a five-minute conversation can avoid. Don't be afraid to schedule a quick chat if you and the reviewers aren't seeing eye-to-eye.

Incorporating Feedback

If you end up needing to make changes to the code based on the review, make those as a separate diff so that the reviewer can see just the changes you've made, and not have to re-review the entire thing.

Roadblocks

No one to review/non-substantive review.

If your team doesn't have a culture of code review, it may be difficult to find someone to do it. You may also get review feedback that isn't useful or complete.

Other than asking nicely or promising something in return, this is a tough situation and you may need to go forward without having the code reviewed. Hopefully, your team lead will look over the changes before promoting them to the main codebase, but they are likely going to be too busy to give it close scrutiny.

The best thing you can do in this situation is to spend at least a day away from your changes and re-read them after that short break. The code will appear somewhat fresh and you might find some issues that you wouldn't normally see after working with the code for several days.

Persistent discussions on style/approach.

I had a code review once where the reviewer took issue with a stylistic decision I had made. It had nothing to do with the underlying change or the correctness of the system. It was a classic "agree to disagree" situation and, as I was the maintainer of the codebase, I kept the change the way I had done it. He complained to my boss, who then directed me to change it. Not cool.

You may encounter a similar situation when having your code reviewed. You may find that the reviewer is insistent that you do things "their way". This is a difficult situation, especially if the other developer is either senior to you or more experienced.

The first thing you should do in this situation is re-think the change. Ask yourself if the reviewer has a point and if there really is something substantially wrong about the code in question. Chances are, the reviewer is right.

If you are not convinced of this, ask the reviewer to explain in more technical terms why you should make the change they are suggesting. Explain that you don't see anything substantially wrong and that, as the code's maintainer, you feel your style should be given more weight. This might either defuse the situation or lead to a deeper discussion of why the code is problematic.

In the end, the reviewer may just forget about your code, but if the person is persistent and presents roadblocks, you might need to just make their suggested changes just to move on. In the end, it's more valuable to ship your code than to "be right" in a code review. If you end up taking this route, I'd recommend you avoid including this person in future code reviews.

4.7 Commit Your Changes

Once your code is reviewed, you'll want to prepare your commit. Depending on the version control system you are using, and the policies of your team, you may have multiple commits that were created as you did your work, or you may have one large commit. Ideally, you have one large commit so that each line you touched will be associated with a single message.

If you are using a version control system that handles merges well (such as Git) it might be OK to leave your commits as they are. In this case, you can put your message in the merge commit's message.

Your message is similar to the one you wrote for your code review guidance and based on the guidelines outlined in section 3.6. Include a summary of what the feature does and why it exists, with a link to the full requirements document.

If you made significant changes to existing classes, call those out and document why those changes were necessary. You want to create an artifact for future developers. When they are looking at a line of code and see that you modified it, they will bring up the commit message. Include anything that they might find useful.

4.8 How to Report Progress

With simple bugfixes, there's typically no expectation to report progress; either you're working on the bugfix or it's done. Here, you might be working for several days or even weeks, depending on the complexity of the task. Simply stating that you are "in progress" isn't helpful and project stakeholders deserve more visibility.

That being said, you don't want to indicate some percentage complete, or some number of hours left to work if you can help it. Instead, I'd report progress as a status, based on where you are in the process:

- In steps one through four, if you haven't started coding, your status is "understanding the problem".

- In step five, your status is "coding" or "in progress". While it's OK to describe how far along you are within this step, resist making promises. A lot can happen in just a few hours' coding. A good tactic here is to comment on the feature in your feature management system (or report at a regular status meeting if your team does them) with what you've done or what you plan to work on next, but with no indication of any level of completeness. This demonstrates progress, but without setting expectations.

- In steps six and seven, your status is "in review".

These three "statuses" should give enough visibility to how far along you are without giving any false impressions or hard-to-keep promises.

Once you've committed your changes, you might not yet be done. Depending on how your team promotes changes to production, you may need to take extra steps to make sure the change goes up.

If you practice some form of "continuous delivery" where changes are promoted when they are ready, you can simply promote your change to production by whatever means your team has established. If features are delivered in batch on a regular schedule (e.g. every week), then you likely don't need to do anything else (although I would double-check that the feature made it to production at the next scheduled release date).

4.9 Moving On

Although it took quite a few pages to describe this process, don't think of it as a stifling, bureaucratic, or rigid methodology. Instead, think of it as a way to get organized. It's a repeatable process for delivering results quickly, correctly, and cleanly.

With this process, you can tackle most programming tasks you'll face on a regular basis. Although it's designed to deliver maintainable and clean code, it isn't fool-proof; coding is still a human process. Decisions that seem correct now, might seem wrong upon further reflection. More likely, the conditions under which you wrote your code might change. New requirements, changing priorities, or other unforeseeable events might occur. The software becomes "crufty".

Sometimes cruft can be avoided by more careful refactoring, but other times, cruft is the result of carefully chosen compromises needed to meet a deadline or other requirement. Many developers conflate these two concepts, but as a senior developer, you have to know the difference between technical debt and slop. This is the subject of the next chapter.

5

Deal With Technical Debt and Slop

At this point, you have a process to handle most programming tasks you'd be given on an average day. From bug-fixing, to small features, to larger features, you should be able to deliver results quickly and easily.

Despite your best efforts, code can begin to *rot* and become "crufty". Over time, the design of certain parts of our application will begin to hinder our ability to change it. Many developers call code like this *technical debt*. The reality is that sometimes sloppy code is just sloppy and could've been easily avoided. I call this *slop*, and this chapter is about understanding the difference.

5.1 Slop: Code to Fix Now

You're under the gun to deliver a feature quickly and you've just gotten your acceptance-level test to pass. Your code has unit test coverage and you feel confident that the system works. But, to do so, you had to copy and paste a lot of business logic, your variable names aren't very good, and you've created a few new public APIs that are poorly documented and counter-intuitive. Should you ship this code?

No.

The reason is that you can fix these problems before the code has a chance to infect the rest of the system. All of these issues are not only fixable, but *quickly* fixable. Removing copy and paste code, renaming variables, and documenting APIs is straightforward, and can often be done in less time than it takes to discuss whether or not you should even do them! Depending on your language and toolchain, you could fix some of these issues with the click of a button.

Code that has these sorts of issues is called *slop* because it's sloppy and can be fixed quickly. Slop is also indicated by poor test coverage, missing error handling, inconsistent use of logging, or a lack of validation of assumptions. Slop exists mainly because you didn't spend enough time refactoring. Slop is complexity that *you've* introduced and that you can easily fix.

Don't feel too bad about it. The process of writing software is a human one and no developer can churn out perfectly clean code every time. The entire reason we separate refactoring into its own step is to allow us to focus on issues just like these. So when you see slop, take a few minutes to clean it up.

Let's look at an example.

Suppose we have a Customer class, a Product class, and an Order class. Each of these represents analogous domain objects: A customer purchases a product, creating an order representing that purchase.

Suppose that the system's Order class has a method that can determine if the customer should be able to purchase a particular Product for free, based on the customer's existing store credit, other discounts, and the price of the product. That code looks like so (if you aren't familiar with Ruby, see appendix D.1 for a *very* brief overview of how to read Ruby code):

```ruby
class Product
  def price
    @price
  end
end

class Order

  # ...

  def free?
    (self.customer.store_credit +
     self.discounts_applied) >= self.product.price
  end

end
```

The method `free?` returns a boolean based on comparing the sum of the order's customer's `store_credit` and the order's discounts against the price of the order's product. This is the current state of the system.

You now need to implement a new feature where the customer is shown that a product they might purchase would be free, based on the store credit they have. Further, the customer might have applied a discount code during the ordering process, so we want to take that into account as well.

Because the customer needs to see this information before a purchase is created, you can't re-use the `free?` method on Order directly because there is no order yet.

After writing your tests, you get things working as quickly as you can which, in this case, means copying the code from Order and tweaking it slightly.

```
class Product

  # ...

  def free_for_customer?(customer,code)
    discounts = 0
    if !code.nil?
      discounts = code.discount_amount
    end
    (customer.store_credit + discounts) >=
      self.price
  end
end
```

The tests pass, and the feature technically works, but it's less than ideal. Not only have you copied code from somewhere else, you've modified it slightly so the duplicated business logic isn't apparent. Anyone creating future features related to discounting and store credit will have to change both of these blocks of code, assuming they realize that both duplicate the same business logic. Further, the variable code is not very well-named. It should be discount_code, but you were in a hurry.

Many developers, if they are feeling pressured to complete their work, would call this an acceptable compromise, promise to fix it later, and ship it. This code is slop and, as a senior developer, you shouldn't ship it. You only need a few minutes to clean it up, which will save much more time than that down the road.

All you need to do is extract a method to encapsulate the discounting logic somewhere accessible to both Product and Order. Since every Order has a Product, you can put this new method in Product. You call it purchase_free? and have it take the customer and any discounts that were applied.

```
class Product
  def free_for_customer?(customer,discount_code)
    discounts = 0
    if !discount_code.nil?
      discounts = discount_code.discount_amount
    end

    purchase_free?(customer,discounts)
  end

  def purchase_free?(customer,discounts)
    (customer.store_credit + discounts) >=
      self.price
  end
end

class Order
  def free?
    self.product.purchase_free?(
      self.customer,
      self.discounts_applied)
  end
end
```

The copy and paste code is now gone (as is the bad variable name) and it took *maybe* five minutes to fix. There is now exactly one place where the logic related to discounting lives and no one would be confused by how it works. This code is clean, maintainable, and shippable. It is no longer slop. Since all of the tests are still passing, you can be sure that this change is a good one and didn't break anything.

That being said, there are still some issues with this code. Does discounting logic really belong in the Product class? It's a convenient place to put it, but it seems out of place. If a future feature needs to calculate a discount, but doesn't have a Product instance, it's going to be hard to re-use this logic. Imaginary features like this can lead to over-engineering and the phrase "You Aren't Gonna Need It" can keep your imagination in check.

Still, what if such a feature did come up? It's hard to argue that our code is now slop simply because of a new requirement. The reality is that we made a design decision based on the state of the world at the time and, if world changes, our once clean code would make it difficult to change the system. This is a form of *technical debt.*

5.2 Technical Debt: Code to Fix Later (or Never)

Technical Debt is a wonderful term, coined by Ward Cunningham, used to explain compromises in implementation that save cost now, at a larger future cost (just like real debt). Unlike slop, which is bad code we can fix immediately and quickly, technical debt is code written under certain assumptions that no longer hold.

In the case of the discounting logic, the assumption was that the logic was needed in only two places. A new feature has violated this assumption making the code technical debt.

More common, however, is knowingly acquiring technical debt, based on an assumption that might hold now, but will certainly not hold in the future. In this case, we *are* "gonna need it", but we're choosing to ignore that fact to meet a deadline.

It's important to understand that technical debt can be a good thing. One of the main reasons we talked about slop first was to make a clear distinction between "poorly written code" and "code that makes a tradeoff". Technical debt is a way to deliver results when they're needed, making tradeoffs in a controlled way. Although you'll likely need to pay it off someday, you might not *necessarily* have to.

Let's see an example.

Part of the discounting logic had the notion of a discount code, something the user might type into their shopping cart to get a discount as part of a promotion. Suppose the Order class has a method that applies this discount code, like so:

```
class DiscountCode
  def amount
    @amount
  end
end

class Order
  def apply_discount_code(discount_code)
    self.discounts_applied += discount_code.amount
  end
end
```

The company has several big promotions scheduled, but wants discount codes to be restricted by the country of an order's shipping address. For example, if I have a US discount code, I shouldn't be able to use that to order something and ship it to Ireland.

Suppose further that a separate team has built a discount code service that ensures a particular code is valid and hasn't already been used. This service should include the shipping-address restriction logic, but the team is behind schedule and they won't be able to deliver it in time for launch. To make matters worse, there's no way to tell the "country" of a discount code; this service was supposed to expose it, but the feature isn't ready yet.

In order to launch in time for the promotion, you have to work around this problem. As it happens, this promotion is for the US only, so you know that all discount codes are US-based. This means that any shipping address outside the US can't use a discount code.

Although this compromise allows you to launch on time, this code will certainly require rework when you launch promotions in other countries. This is technical debt.

Let's look at the implementation:

```
class DiscountCodeService
  def self.valid?(discount_code)
    # Code to talk to external discount code
    # service - currently just checks if
    # the code is valid and has not
    # been used
  end
end

class DiscountCode

  # ...

  def applicable?(shipping_address)
    # TECHDEBT: We dont have promotions running
    # in other countries and the discount code
    # service doesnt yet have the ability to
    # validate codes against shipping countries,
    # so we hard-code it to launch on time.
    # This needs to be fixed before we run
    # promotions outside the US
    DiscountCodeService.valid?(self.code) &&
      shipping_address.country.code == "US"
```

```
    end
end

class Order
  def apply_discount_code(code)
    if code.applicable?(self.shipping_address)
      self.discounts_applied += code.amount
      true
    else
      logger.warn "#{code} cannot be applied!"
      false
    end
  end
end
```

Although this code is clean and shippable, it incurs technical debt. The second we run a promotion outside the US, this code breaks. What's important about this code is that we've called it out as technical debt.

The annotated comment is a message to other developers that we weren't being lazy, but that we knowingly did something less than ideal because we needed to ship. Also note that the annotated comment includes a test for when this code must be fixed.

Further, since comment is annotated with TECHDEBT:, you can run static analysis of the codebase (or simply do a text search on it) to bring up a list of technical debts you've incurred.

It's also important that this information is in a code comment and not just in the commit message. We want developers reading this code to immediately see that, not only is this code technical debt, but *why* the debt had to be incurred. A developer isn't going to be guaranteed to chase through the commit history to find out why this code is written this way, assuming the developer even asks the question.

You will likely need to "pay down" this technical debt. When you are forming your implementation plan for a future feature (as described in section 4.4), you'll note areas explicitly called out as technical debt as well as parts of the code that will need significant changes in light of the new requirements (such as the discounting logic from section 5.2).

In these cases, you'll want to "pay down" the debt before you start adding new features. You'll also likely need to inform your team lead, project manager, or stakeholder that your task will take a bit longer because your debt has now come due. This is why the term is so effective, because even the least technical person on the team will understand what you mean when you say it.

We've mentioned a few times that it's entirely possible that you never have to pay down a particular debt. In a sense, this is part of the "bet" you are taking by acquiring the debt in the first place. In our example, suppose our promotions are a flop, and we never roll them out in other countries. In this case, there's zero value in paying down the debt we acquired. We'd be implementing a feature we'll never use. It also validates our decision to incur the debt and ship, rather than delay the initial promotion to build a feature we didn't end up needing.

5.3 Moving On

The phrase "Technical debt" is just one example of how developers can effectively communicate with non-technical people in an honest way. It's important to be able to allow others to make sound business decisions without having to understand all the details of how a particular software system works. In the next chapter, we'll expand on the concept of communication and learn how you can effectively communicate with others.

6

Play Well With Others

One of the hardest challenges you'll face as a programmer is to explain what you do, or how you've done it, to someone who is not a programmer. It's even more challenging when the person to whom you are explaining needs this information to make a business decision.

Translating your work to non-technical people is a skill that can be more valuable than any specific technical knowledge you have. It's what makes a senior developer in the eyes of others.

Effective communication about technical details isn't just about "non-technical" managers or executives. For example, a company's Chief Technology Officer (CTO) will be incredibly knowledgeable about technology, but will lack the context to understand the issues at hand (context they shouldn't need to always have in order to do their job). Technical or not, communicating with other people still has the same challenge: distill technical information such that it can be easily understood.

The first step is to empathize with your audience. If you can feel what it's like to have to make a decision without detailed information, it can go a long way to communicating such information yourself. Next, you'll need to distill what you know in a way your audience can understand.

We'll talk about both of these in detail, including some specific tips, before reading an example scenario where these tips are put to use.

6.1   Empathize With Your Audience

Your manager, other users, project stakeholders, or even your team lead need to apply your expertise to a problem. This is the essence of being a software engineer. Typically, these "interested parties" understand the problem more deeply than you, but lack the technical knowledge, skill, or time to solve it directly. They also have their own sets of priorities and constraints, most of which you won't be aware of.

This situation is not unique to software development. If you think about it, there are many situations where *you* are the one in need of expertise. Have you ever undergone a major medical procedure? Ever worked with an accountant or lawyer? Hired a contractor get work done on your home?

In each of these examples, *you* are the "non-technical" decision maker who needs to apply external expertise to solve a problem.

Several years ago, I was in need of minor back surgery. I had a "herniated disc", a term I didn't really understand. The doctor put it simply: "there's a sack of fluid that sits between your vertebrae. Two of them have ruptured, which is causing your back to rub against a particular nerve, which is why you are in pain. We can go in and clean out the parts of these sacks that are causing problems. This should alleviate the pain."

Although this wasn't enough information to get me through even five minutes of medical school, it explained the problem and the proposed solution in terms that I could understand. I was now able to make an important decision - whether or not to undergo surgery - without having to first get a medical degree.

This is the position your managers and other company decision-makers are in. Not only do they not know how to do what you do, but they often don't even have the vocabulary to know what to ask for. Further, they likely don't know what they don't know and will have a lot of wrong assumptions about what software development is. Finally, their priorities and job pressures won't be obvious to you, but will play a big role in how they approach you to help solve a problem.

This isn't necessarily a fault on their part, however. Not everyone can know everything in great detail. Instead of thinking of them as "pointy-haired bosses", think of them as partners. They understand the problem and you know how to solve it. This "division of labor" is why teams can achieve greater things than any individual.

That being said, not everyone operates from the same set of priorities (something we'll discuss in more detail in chapter 7). Part of the reason that the first step in writing code from the previous chapters was to "understand the problem" is to make sure that the results you're being asked to deliver are actually valuable.

Part of your job is to push back when you're being asked to solve the wrong problem. Often, having the types of discussions we're talking about here can help you identify the real underlying problem your team needs to solve. It's often not what you've been initially asked to do.

Empathizing with the other person can go a long way, but you'll eventually need to convey the information in question. To do this, you must put it into terms the other person will understand, and summarize the details as much as you can. I call this *adapting* and *abstracting*.

6.2 Adapt and Abstract Information

To tackle the problem of communication with others, we can apply some lessons from software development. Think of the information you have as a highly flexible, very detailed API. Your manager or product owner wants to consume that API, but doesn't need every feature it provides, nor do they have time to process the detailed information coming back. They need a simpler API.

To do this, you'd create an *adapter* to the complex API and would *abstract* away the details. Your new API won't have the power or depth of the original, but it will be vastly simpler to use and easier to understand.

Communicating with other people isn't exactly like writing software, but the analogy gets us close. We want to adapt our terms to theirs, and we want to abstract away irrelevant information as much as we can.

Adapt Terms

"Jargon", "Lingo", and "bizspeak" can be frustrating for a developer to have to deal with. It can seem that everyone else is speaking a foreign language at times. Although you might be able to teach your co-workers some of your terminology, you'll have much greater success adapting your terms and concepts to ones they already understand.

My wife and I frequently visit Puerto Rico for vacation. Although most Puerto Ricans speak English, the vast majority speak Spanish as their first language. My wife is fluent in Spanish, which makes it a lot easier for us while we're there. When communicating with others, you need to learn how to speak the language.

Here are some tips to help you adapt your terms to someone else's:

- Avoid technical jargon of your own. At best, your audience won't understand the words you're using at all. Worse, they'll *think* they understand the meaning of a common word that actually means something completely different.

- Listen carefully to the words people use and ask questions if you aren't 100% sure what they mean. You might feel silly asking such questions, but you'll feel a lot sillier when you can't get your point across.

- Don't "talk down". The other person is likely a highly intelligent person who is capable of understanding what you're explaining. Treating them like a child will only make things worse.

- Don't be afraid to use longer descriptive phrases in place of acronyms or other jargon. For example, you might prefer to use the phrase "the list of users waiting to be activated" instead of "the user-ack queue".

Once you have a handle on the terms you'll be using, you must next distill your information into a simpler form that's easier to understand: abstraction.

Abstract Concepts to Simplify Them

When explaining a new concept, you want to keep things simple and straightforward. Start out slowly, painting broad strokes. Avoid edge cases, at least initially, as they can create confusion and distraction. Often, the other party will ask about edge cases themselves. This is a good sign that they are understanding you.

I'm not recommending you hide details, or make an approach or concept look better (or worse) than it is, but you

81

need to distill your message to its absolute minimum without giving out false information.

For example, you might be integrating with a third-party service that geo-codes addresses. Although this service is extremely reliable, it's not *100%* reliable. There's no need to get into this nuance initially. It's sufficient to state that the geo-coding service is reliable enough to be integrated into the existing application.

Once the basics are understood, you may need to give more details or touch on some of the edge cases. Use the other person as a guide but don't be afraid to ask a few questions to test their understanding. This is especially important when you haven't built a strong rapport with the other person. The trust needed to rely on your summaries hasn't been built, yet.

Here are some tips to help abstract information so that others can more easily understand it:

- Avoid technical details.

- Explain things using analogies; don't worry about precision.

- Use diagrams, visual aids, or demonstrations where possible.

- Always offer to provide more details.

- If a question has taken you off course, spend a few seconds re-establishing the context of your discussion. For example, "OK, so we were talking about how the files we get from the shipping vendor are placed on their private FTP site, and our background job downloads them every hour. The next step is..."

- Be prepared to "justify" your position if challenged. Do this by gradually increasing the level of detail. This is especially important if you are delivering "bad news".

You should feel free to stop frequently and take questions or make sure that everyone understands what you're saying. Remember, it's not the other person's job to understand you, it's your job to make sure they understand. If you aren't getting through, assume it's because you can do a better job.

Don't be afraid to stop and re-group if things are going poorly. Find a colleague you trust or respect who can (or already does) understand the technical information in question and ask how they would handle it.

Finally, be wary of solving the wrong problem. Often, people will come to the developers asking about a specific solution rather than explaining the underlying problem. Organizations that excessively "shield" developers from others encourage this behavior, as staff are trained to "not bother" the developers. In this case, stop and ask what the real problem is. In many cases, the best solution to their problem is not the one they initially asked for.

Let's see how this approach serves us in an example scenario.

6.3   Example

Suppose your company wants its support staff to be able to generate a wide variety of recurring and ad-hoc reports based on the database of your application. Monica, the head of the support staff, heard about a software package called OneNine that she thinks might work. Your boss Vick asks you to look into it. Monica wants to know what the cost of implementing this software package will be, since it will need to pull data from your application's database.

Being familiar with the data, and having a vague notion of the kinds of reporting that needs to be done, you pore over the documentation for OneNine - even downloading a demo - to try it out. Your application's database is in a fully-normalized set of relational tables. OneNine requires data to be in STAR Schemas. A STAR schema is used for reporting and analysis and is typically generated from the more definitive normalized store. There's currently no process to translate your database into a STAR schema and you aren't sure if anyone has the bandwidth to set it up and maintain it.

Monica and Vick need to make a decision. Should they purchase OneNine or look at other packages? Vick is technical enough that you could certainly explain it to him so *he* could explain it to Monica, but if she has questions, Vick won't have the answers. You really need to be able to explain it yourself. Of course, Monica is not a technical manager and doesn't know what third-normal form is, what a STAR schema does, or how to translate data from one to the other; she just wants her reports.

You schedule a meeting with Vick and Monica and get right to the point:

"The way we store data is not in a format compatible with OneNine. We'll need to write a translation process between our format and the one OneNine expects, plus we'll have to have someone on staff assigned to monitor and support this process. It's not a full-time job, but it's critical enough that we'll need to make sure someone owns it."

This explanation is a nice summary of the situation, contains no jargon, and is concise yet accurate. This isn't what Monica was hoping to hear, so she asks a frustrating, yet completely innocent, question:

"OneNine says they support Oracle, and we're using Oracle. Isn't that sufficient?"

This is the problem with summarizing. You've used the word "format" to mean "schema" (a concept Monica has likely never even heard of) and Monica has understood "format" as "database vendor", the only piece of information she has about databases.

You try to explain:

"All that means is that they can make a network connection to any Oracle database. That's different than actually interpreting the data inside the database. To do that, it expects the data to be in a specific format, and it's not a format we're using."

Monica shows no signs of understanding. At this point, showing might be more effective than telling, so you fire up your spreadsheet application and open a blank workbook. Like most computer-savvy professionals, Monica understands what a spreadsheet does and how to use it.

In your blank spreadsheet, you type in the following table:

Day	Lem	Ronnie	Julian
Monday	5.6	3.4	8.4
Tuesday	5.6	3.4	8.4
Wednesday	5.6	3.4	8.4
Thursday	5.6	3.4	8.4
Friday	5.6	3.4	8.4

You then select the table and generate a graph. You explain:

"Suppose that this graph is OneNine, which is showing us the hours worked per employee per day. Suppose that this table is the format in which OneNine expects data. Everything works great, and the graph shows us what we want. Now, suppose *our* data looks like this:"

You open up a new sheet and enter in the data:

Employee	M	T	W	Th	F
Lem	5:20	6:45	8:00	3:34	8:15
Ronnie	5:20	6:45	8:00	3:34	8:15
Julian	5:20	6:45	8:00	3:34	8:15

You continue:

"If I were to ask OneNine to graph this data, which I could do by just copying it over the data in the other sheet, the graph wouldn't work at all. The data is structured differently *and* the values are encoded differently. OneNine has decimals, where we have strings representing hours and minutes."

Monica is starting to understand. You continue:

"We'd need a piece of software to turn the row-based data into OneNine's column-based data, while simultaneously translating the strings into decimals. I'm simplifying quite a bit here, so you can imagine how complex something like this would be in the real world."

With a visual aid in a program that Monica has used, she gets it.

"Ah! That makes sense. But why wouldn't we just store our data in their format? Then both programs would work, and we wouldn't need a translation process."

Another innocent, yet frustrating question.

"Our data is stored in a way that's simplest for the application to work with. Switching how we store it would be orders of magnitude more work than writing a translation program. Like I said, the translation program isn't a full-time job, though it's also not trivial either."

Sensing a common understanding on both sides, Vick jumps in:

"It looks like we have our answer. We'll need a developer for, say, a month or two to set up the translation layer, and then a few hours per week of ongoing support. Monica, we'll need someone on your end as a liaison, but it looks like we have our answer."

Monica nods in response: "Great, that's all I need to know. I'll let you all know if we intend to go forward or if we have other packages to evaluate. Thanks for your time!"

Job well done. Monica was able to make a decision, and she didn't have to learn about database schemas, normalization, or encoding formats. You were able to adapt your terms to hers, summarize what you found out, and give relevant details as needed to help her understand.

6.4 Moving On

Learning to abstract and adapt technical information for others can be tough, but it's a skill that will make you stand out from others who can't. Being able to "talk the talk" with others can make you more effective and more valuable to your company. Being able to briefly summarize technical details even more so.

Non-technical co-workers aren't your toughest audience when communicating, however, other developers are. You'll find yourself in many situations where you need to explain or convince other developers to make a technical decision or justify one you've made. Since developers *can* get into all the nitty-gritty details, you have to be prepared. In the next chapter, we'll talk about how to make a convincing technical argument.

7

Make Technical Decisions

There's usually more than one way to apply software to solve a particular problem. Making a decision about what solution to use can be difficult; programmers are an opinionated bunch. When the decision is personal, discussing the options is more sport than profession (such as the age-old "Editor War" between vim and emacs). Most of the time, however, the decision about how to solve a business problem affects everyone on the team (or everyone in the company).

As you advance in your career, you will be responsible for making more and more decisions about how you and your team work. You may also find yourself needing approval from others about a technology or technique you wish to use. In these situations, being able to defend your decisions and make a reasoned technical argument is crucial.

At a high level, you must identify facts (as distinct from opinions), identify your priorities (as well as the priorities of others) and then combine the two in order to make your decision or put forth your argument. You need to learn how to debate effectively, even if it's just with yourself.

7.1   Identify Facts

Facts (more formally, "propositions") are pieces of information about the topic of discussion that can be verified. Facts are not up for debate (although their importance certainly is; we'll get to that). For example, "Java is a compiled language" is a fact, whereas, "compilation slows down the development process" is not (nor is "compilation speeds up the development process").

Of course, the facts you must consider aren't always so cut and dried. Consider the phrase "the development team feels that compilation slows them down". Although it's not clear that compilation is actually slowing the team down (and thus is not a fact), it's true that the team has this particular feeling. You could easily verify it by polling the members of the team in question. If a majority feel that compilation slows them down, then you've identified a fact about the team, not about compilation.

Opinions like this are often indicators of hidden facts that you have yet to identify. Ideally, you can replace facts about a team or person's feelings with facts about the matter at hand.

For example, you might discover that the compiler compiles every source file every time, rather than compiling only those files that are out-of-date. *This* is a fact and would certainly explain why the team feels compilation slows them down. This fact could also lead you to investigate further and uncover other facts, such as "incremental compilation isn't possible for this project" or "the latest version of the compiler now supports incremental compilation".

However you get there, you want to be very clear what are facts and what are opinions. As we'll see, priorities - what's important to whom - applied to facts are the basis of a convincing argument.

While you're identifying facts, you should also start to understand the priorities of everyone involved, including yourself. As we'll see, identifying what's important to different people can lead you to the pursuit of additional facts.

7.2 Identify Priorities

Priorities are a list of what's important to someone, either in general, or with respect to the decision at hand. For example, one of your boss' priorities might be to hire as many competent developers as possible to help the company grow. You will use the priorities of everyone involved in a decision to give weight to the various facts you've identified.

In a sense, priorities themselves are facts and all we're doing is using inferences to draw conclusions, however I find the distinction here useful. Facts, in the way I'm describing them here, are about *things* whereas priorities are about *people*. Because of this, it can be easy to overlook priorities, since they are more difficult to ascertain than simply reading documentation or playing around with code.

Explicitly identifying priorities can make your decisions, and the discussion around them, more straightforward than aimlessly arguing about the importance of the various facts. Even if you are just making a decision on your own, identifying priorities is a good "gut check".

Equally useful to your priorities are the priorities of others involved in the discussion. When you are making a persuasive argument, you will be more effective when you understand what's important to the other person. For example, your boss' priorities might include the desire to move developers easily between projects. This priority is going to give weight to a fact like "most projects at the company are written using Rails".

If you know (or have a good guess) at the other party's priorities, write those down next to yours when figuring our your argument. If you aren't sure, it's often helpful to just simply ask. You want to form a "virtual personality" of the people involved in the discussion, so you can have a sense of how they will react and what information they need.

As you explore everyone's priorities, you'll likely uncover more facts or areas for investigation. For example, the system administrator assigned to your team might have as a priority "I need to monitor the memory usage of all applications on the systems I maintain". If you haven't investigated the memory usage of some new application server you're proposing, your argument isn't going to resonate with your sysadmin (and you can't expect your sysadmin to do your fact-finding for you).

Once you've got the facts identified and understand everyone's priorities, including your own, you should be able to draw some conclusions.

7.3   Draw Conclusions

As mentioned, each priority gives weight to the importance of the facts. For each fact, ask yourself how much it matters to you, given your priorities. Do the same for each person whose priorities you've identified, e.g. how much would the boss really care about the fact that Haskell allows pure functional programming?.

Hopefully, you'll have identified facts that speak to everyone's priorities and lead everyone to the same conclusion. If that's the case, your job is mostly done. If not, this means that some priorities are conflicting. Resolving these conflicts should be the subject of an in-person discussion and it should be highly focused because of all the legwork you've done.

Let's see an example.

7.4   Example

Suppose you are the team lead of a new project, and you've decided that Node, a relatively new JavaScript-based application framework, is the best fit for the project. You don't get to make that decision on your own: you've got to convince your manager Vick and the Ops lead, Danny. Danny and her team are responsible for maintaining applications in production.

The Facts So Far

- Node is a JavaScript-based web application framework.

- The project team knows JavaScript and Node already (most of the team have used Node for side projects).

- Most developers at the company know JavaScript.

- Learning a framework based on a language you know is simpler than learning one based on a new language.

- Almost all existing applications at the company are based on Ruby on Rails.

- The Ops team has no experience deploying Node applications.

- Using a new framework will be fun, boosting morale, and making the project more enjoyable to work on.

- A happy team is more productive than an unhappy team.

Priorities

Your priorities are:

- The business must be successful.

- The team should use the technology that's the best fit for the task at hand.

- Features should be delivered as quickly as possible.

Vick's priorities are:

- The business must be successful.

- Projects should succeed at delivering business value.

- Developers should be happy in their currently assigned work and in working for Vick.

- Developers should be re-assignable to different projects, without excessive ramp-up time, if needed for business reasons.

Danny's priorities are:

- The business must be successful.

- It should be as simple as possible to manage the production environment.

- All applications must be monitored and their logs aggregated easily.

- The Ops team members should be generalists and able to support any part of the production environment. This ensures that productions systems aren't significantly affected by vacations, sickness, or attrition.

Notice how each person's priorities, given the same set of facts, can lead to different conclusions? Danny would be crazy to agree to support a Node application. The facts you've identified are biased toward your priorities and, to a lesser extent, Vick's.

More Fact-Finding

Before taking your case to Danny, you decide to do some more investigation. You need some facts that address Danny's priorities more directly. After talking to your fellow developers and reading some documentation, you identify some additional relevant facts:

- Node applications can easily be configured to log in the same way a Rails app logs.

- Node requires system libraries consistent with what's installed on existing production machines.

- Node applications can be managed with Monit, the tool Ops is currently using to manage the few non-Rails apps in production.

You can now approach your discussion with Danny from a much stronger and more reasonable viewpoint. Instead of having your argument shot-down immediately ("No one in ops knows anything about Node, so I'm sorry, but we don't have the capacity right now"), you can debate priorities.

Drawing Conclusions

Danny can see that deploying Node isn't that foreign. The logging and process management features of Node are consistent with what's already deployed and no new system software needs to be installed to support the Node runtime. Although this doesn't change the fact that more types of applications make Danny's job more difficult, it makes Node a lot more palatable.

Notice how "The business must be successful" is a priority that everyone shares? Making that explicit helps underscore the point that everyone's on the same team and, at the end of the day, is working toward the same goal. Because of this, a decision to disallow Node might have a negative impact on the business as a whole.

Given all of these facts, Danny agrees to try out deploying a simple Node app as a test in the next few days. If everything goes smoothly, she'll sign off on supporting it in production.

Of course, not all debates are going to go this smoothly; the human mind is a lot less objective than a computer. Sometimes a convincing argument fails to convince or, worse, an unconvincing argument wins the day. Whether it's your own argument, or those of others, you need to be aware of logical fallacies. These can lead smart people to draw the wrong conclusions.

7.5 Fallacies

According to Wikipedia, a logical fallacy is:

> an error in reasoning often due to a misconception or a presumption.

You need to be familiar with these fallacies and identify them when you hear them. Making decisions based on unsound reasoning can create problems later on and fallacies have a way of cropping up in many debates. Well-intentioned and intelligent people mistakenly use them all the time.

The Wikipedia page is a good resource to use, however the following are some I've noticed in particular to technology-related debates:

Hasty Generalization Arguing from a special case to a general rule, e.g. "I worked on one project using Clojure, and it was a disaster, therefore we should not use Clojure."

Straw Man Misrepresenting the facts or conclusions and then arguing against them, e.g. "JavaScript has numerous browser incompatibilities, therefore it is unsuitable for server-side applications."

No true Scotsman Given a counterexample, modify the assertion via rhetoric, e.g. "No sane programmer would use threads". The term comes from philosopher Antony Flew who illustrated the fallacy via an anecdote about an outraged Scotsman reading about crimes committed by other Scotsman. The outraged Scotsman remarked that "no true Scotsman" would act that way.

Composition Assuming that the something true about the parts will apply to the whole, e.g. "Process-based concurrency is easy to understand, and Resque is an easy-to-understand queueing system, therefore our process-based Rails app that uses Resque will be easy to understand."

Correlation does not imply Causation Concluding that correlated actions must somehow cause one or the other, e.g. "At 10am when we send out bulk emails, the public website experiences slowness, therefore the bulk email job is causing the website to be slow."

False Equivalence Concluding that two statements are true because they share similar aspects, e.g. "Ruby and Python are both scripting languages, so it doesn't matter which one we use for doing quantitative analysis".

Appeal to Authority Attempting to assert something because a respected or intelligent person has asserted it, possibly in a different context, e.g. "Linus Torvalds says C++ is horrible, therefore we should never use C++."

I have seen very smart developers use all these fallacies. I've used them, too. Understanding them is important because humans aren't perfect, logical reasoning machines. We also tend to rely on intuition, especially when objectively correct answers can't be made from the facts at hand. Identifying fallacies when you hear them will clear up your own reasoning and make sure that you aren't susceptible to it from others. Pointing it out (depending on your level of tact) can also help make sure the smart people around you are reasoning properly as well, thus improving the quality of the entire group's decision making.

If someone remains unconvinced by your arguments, rather than assume the person is "not getting it", take a moment to consider if your argument really is lacking. Give everyone the benefit of the doubt. Is there a fact you got wrong? A priority you haven't identified? Your mission isn't to prove that you are right, it's to deliver the best results you can.

Aside from identifying facts and weighing them based on priorities, it's also important to do some level of documentation around how certain decisions get made.

7.6 Document the Decision-Making Process

Once a decision is made, and you are moving forward, I find it useful to jot down *why* the decision was made. Hopefully you have a shared documentation space, such as a wiki, where something like this can go. Even if you don't, keep this written artifact around.

It doesn't need to be anything grandiose or formalized. You can likely just list the facts and priorities and summarize the discussion around those priorities.

A document like this is useful for two reasons. First, it can prevent someone else from going through the trouble that you've just gone through. Consider if another team wants to use Node on their project: you can save them a some time by sharing your work.

Second, it keeps you from having to remember the details when, six months from now, a new team member asks why things are done a certain way. There are few answers more discouraging from a team lead or senior developer than "I don't know", "I don't remember", or "Danny wouldn't let us".

Answers like this are useless at best and disrespectful at worst. By keeping track of the decisions you're involved with, you can give a better answer, such as "Danny felt that the additional cost of maintaining Node applications in production was too high, which would put existing applications at risk, so we stuck with Rails".

7.7 Moving On

Technical arguments can get heated. The process outlined here can help keep your head cool and focused on results. By accounting for the priorities of others, you also focus the decision making on the team working toward common goals, rather than setting up an adversarial situation.

Making technical decisions and arguments is something you'll do on occasion as you work through features and bugs, but you'll be doing a lot more of it when creating a new system from scratch. So-called "greenfield" applications require a lot of up-front decision making, so being able to make - and defend - technical decisions is crucial if you're tasked with starting a new project. We'll find out more in the next chapter.

8

Bootstrap a Greenfield System

Working on a brand new application can be a lot of fun. There's no "baggage" from legacy code, no technical debt, and there's a wonderful feeling of freshness when starting an app from scratch.

Along with the excitement of breaking new ground, there is a lot of important work to do to start the app off on the right foot. The mantra "you aren't gonna need it" works great when working with an existing app but with a brand new "greenfield" application, there are several things that you *are* "gonna" need.

The decisions you make about how your application will be set up can have a lasting impact on the app's ultimate success. For example, consider the choice of technology. Nothing affects the app more than this and it's a decision you *have* to make up front.

Everything we've learned up to this point is going to come into play when you find yourself in the enviable - and delicate - position of bootstrapping a new application. As always, you want to deliver results, and to do so quickly.

8.1 Overview

When given a greenfield project, where there is literally no source code, you have two main goals:

- Make sure everyone involved in the project feels good about the initial direction and decisions being made

- Establish a location for developers to start contributing code

To meet the first goal, you'll need to apply your newfound powers of working with others (chapter 6) and making technical decisions (chapter 7). The decisions you make must take into account everyone with an interest in your project. The previous chapter is your guide on how to do this and it's important that you document all of your decisions and why they were made.

The second goal is more complex and is what we'll cover for the remainder of the chapter.

Proponents of agile methodologies might call the activities around this "Iteration Zero" and I think this is a good way of putting it. The term "iteration" establishes that you'll be working in small increments (which we talked about in section 2.3), but the use of "zero" instead of "one" indicates that no direct business value is going to be delivered initially. This iteration belongs to the developers (who are the only group of people I know that start counting at zero).

At the end of iteration zero, you will have a deployable application (that's hopefully also *deployed*), and some basic guidelines for how the application's code should be written. With these two things, developers can start on iteration *one*, which will deliver business value in the form of application features.

Here's an overview of the process:

1. Understand the problem

2. Understand the system's place in the existing technical architecture

3. Choose the technology

4. Outline application architecture

5. Create a deployment checklist

6. Build and deploy a minimum deployable system

7. Add features, deploying after each one is complete

Let's go over each step in more detail. As we've done in some previous chapters, we'll also talk about common roadblocks you'll come up against.

8.2 Understand the problem

This is a frequent refrain of the book, and it may seem obvious, but you can't start writing software or making big decisions until you understand the problem. Iteration zero will involve making many decisions whose effects are lasting. These decisions will be the most difficult to undo if they turn out to be wrong.

Because of this, it is crucial that you understand - and agree with - the reasons for this new application to exist. If you've proposed the application, your job is done. You will have documented your decision, as discussed in section 7.6, and you're ready to proceed.

In the more likely scenario where you've been asked to build this application by someone else, you will need to piece together the "defense" of this decision. More importantly, you'll need to agree with the decision. You do your company a disservice to build an application you don't think needs to exist.

To understand why the application should be built, find answers to these questions:

- What business problems will this application solve?

- Why is the proposed application the best solution to those problems?

- What other solutions were considered?

As you talk to people and find these answers, write everything down. Your team will benefit from understanding the problem the application solves and it's easier to convey as basic documentation.

Roadblocks

No clear answers.

It may be that no one can clearly explain why this new application needs to be built. This is the sign of a dysfunctional environment, but it's sadly all too common.

In this case, you can still move forward but you'll need to make your decisions with more care. Your decisions should be more conservative, and more along the lines of "the way things are done". Your project is already at risk of failing and, if it does, you want to make sure the real reasons are apparent. It will be too easy to blame bold choices such as new technology or new techniques for the project's failure.

Clear answers that you disagree with.

It's possible that you gain a complete understanding of the business problems the application will solve, but disagree that the proposed solution is the best one. In this case, your best option is to propose an alternate solution that you feel addresses the problems better.

If no alternate is obvious, or your proposal is rejected, this may indicate your project is already at risk of failure. Proceed as you would above, making conservative choices.

8.3 Understand the System's Place in the Technical Architecture

Unless this application is the first one ever being built at your company, you will need to account for existing applications and existing infrastructure, otherwise known as the *technical architecture*. Your application will at least need to run alongside these existing systems, but it's more likely that it will need to integrate with them to some extent.

What these other systems are, and how they work, is a major input to your decision-making. For example, suppose your company deploys its applications using a hosted cloud-computing provider. This provider only allows TCP networking; UDP is blocked. This means that any technology that relies on UDP, such as some metrics-logging systems, can't be part of your application.

Your first step is to get a systems view of the technical architecture. Much as you gained a systems view of an application in order to add a new feature to it, you'll need to do the same thing here, but on a larger scale.

Hopefully, there's documentation around that explains this, however you can piece it together pretty quickly by writing out each system or application and taking a few notes.

- What is it called?

- What is its purpose?

- What technologies does it use?

- Who is the point of contact for it?

- Which development team is responsible for it?

- What other applications does it depend on?

With this list, you should now be able to see where your new application fits. The simplest way to get this view is to identify systems from your larger list that your application will need to interact with. For these systems, you will need to dig a bit deeper.

- Will these systems need to change to accommodate yours?

- If so, how will these changes be made? Do you need to coordinate with the other team, or can you simply make the needed changes yourself?

- Will you need to run these systems in development to run your application or is there a shared development instance you can use?

With this information, along with an understanding of the business problem you're solving, you're now ready to make some decisions about the application itself.

8.4 Choose Technology

The decision of what technology to use for your application will have the biggest impact on its success. The choice of technology is usually irreversible, so this decision requires careful thought.

Most companies have a "blessed stack" of technologies that are used for most applications. You'll need to decide if you should use this stack or if you need to diverge. This is where your ability to make reasoned technical decisions will be put to the test.

Using the Blessed Stack

The "blessed stack" is a set of tools and technologies that are used for most applications at your company. It may seem bureaucratic, but there are many good reasons for doing this: developers know how to use it, the operations team knows how to deploy and monitor it, and the entire team has a sense of what does and doesn't work. Using the blessed stack opens you up to the widest possible array of expertise: your co-workers.

Using the blessed stack can also be a politically correct decision. Perhaps you've heard the phrase "no one ever got fired for buying IBM" (or a more recent version about choosing Microsoft products). This means that if things go wrong on your project, people will start looking to place blame. By going with the blessed stack, you can avoid taking (some of) that blame.

Although making decisions based on political factors - as opposed to technical ones - isn't very satisfying, in some organizations, these factors could be important. While the blessed stack might have technical deficiencies, your list of facts and priorities should account for the culture and politics of your company.

If you personally prefer the blessed stack, I would suggest you simply choose that and move on to other decisions. If, on the other hand, you feel that other technology might be a better fit, you will need to heavily defend that decision, both to yourself and to others.

Using a Different Technology

If you think the blessed stack is not going to meet your needs, you'll need to identify something else that does. This might be an uphill battle or you might have a lot of support for using the right tool for the right job. In either case, it is a good idea to defend the decision (even if it's just to yourself). You must answer the question "Why *shouldn't* I use the blessed stack?"

Although the excitement of using new technology is important as it pertains to morale and job happiness, your first duty is to deliver results. Your decision must focus on that above all else. How will a new, un-blessed technology deliver results better or more quickly than the blessed stack?

There are many ways to objectively evaluate technology. Here a few that you should consider:

Fitness for purpose Is the blessed stack a bad fit for the problem you're facing? Is the new technology better?

Performance Is the blessed stack unable to meet the performance requirements of your problem?

Developer Productivity If you get through the initial pain of setup and deployment, will there be gains in developer productivity that outweigh these up-front costs?

Developer Happiness/Staff Retention Will an investment in this technology make the staff overall happier on the project? Will it elevate the status of your organization? This might not be a technical criterion, but it's absolutely worth considering. If your team is "sick and tired" of using the blessed stack, the injection of something new can invigorate them. Using the latest technology can turn otherwise boring tasks into a lot of fun. You shouldn't discount this.

Making this decision is all about identifying facts and priorities. For any fact that works "against" a priority, try to identify other facts that mitigate that risk. For example, your boss may want to allow staff to move between projects. This makes new technology look undesirable. You could mitigate this risk by identifying resources for using the new technology, such as books, online courses, or training programs.

You should be prepared for the worst: it might be that, given the facts, there is no way to justify the technology you'd like to use.

I went through this exercise at a Java shop. I felt using Ruby on Rails would be a better fit for the problem at hand. After much discussion and analysis with the other senior developers, we ultimately decided that sticking with Java was the right decision. I didn't like it, but it **was** the right decision.

There is a third alternative, which is to examine technologies that aren't the "blessed stack", but that sit within the same "ecosystem" as it.

Using Technology from the Same Ecosystem

If you feel the blessed stack won't meet your needs, it's possible that other technology that's similar to it might work, and be an easier sell. For example, if the blessed stack is Spring MVC, Ruby on Rails is a massive change whereas Struts won't be.

The concerns around using new technology usually come down to two factors: the programming language and the deployment model. The reason that Spring MVC and Rails are so different is that they use different languages (Java vs. Ruby) and are deployed differently (installing a .war file into a container vs. managing a UNIX process).

If you can find an alternative that uses the same programming language and same deployment model as the blessed

ANTADED

stack, you might find that alternative to be a good fit for your project.

For example, writing a Rails app in JRuby[1] affords the same deployment model as a JEE application, which might work well for a Java shop. Writing an application using Sinatra, which uses Ruby and has the same deployment model as a Rails app, might work for a Rails shop.

Keeping Abreast of New Technology

As senior developers, we must choose technology wisely and this is more often than not the "blessed stack". But we must also keep up with the latest tools, techniques, languages, and frameworks. These two mandates are often at odds with one another and can be difficult to reconcile. Further, it can be difficult to come to a deep understanding of a new technology without "using it in anger", i.e. applying it to a real, complex problem.

The main reason *to not* use new or unproven technology is risk. There is a risk that aspects of the technology that only become clear under significant use will contribute to the failure of a project. Of course, not all projects are created equal since the consequences of failure aren't a constant.

The best way to integrate new technology into your repertoire - as well as your team's toolbox - is to find a low-risk project to use as trial. These projects are often simple in nature and aimed at a small group of users who can suffer through some of the instability that comes along with new technologies. If the project fails, you haven't risked much and - even in failure - you'll learn a lot about the technology.

Roadblocks

Blanket requirement to use the blessed stack.

---

[1] JRuby is an implementation of Ruby that runs on the Java Virtual Machine

Some organizations are conservative and no amount of convincing will allow for new, non-blessed technologies to be deployed. It could be that you haven't made your case very well. Re-visit your argument and make sure you considered all the priorities and identified the right facts.

If you feel you've made the best case you can and that the decision-makers are just *wrong*, you won't have many alternatives. In this case, I would recommend keeping detailed notes about your project's rollout. You'll be able to find out for certain if your recommendation would've been better. You may find that you were correct, and it might help shake the company's conservative thinking. You might also find out you were wrong, which will lead to better decision-making in the future.

8.5   Outline the Application's Architecture

You don't need to, nor should you, make a detailed architecture or design for your application up front. You simply don't have all the information you'd need to make all those decisions. That being said, there are some decisions that you know you *will* have to make.

Many of these decisions are around conventions for development. You want your application to ooze consistency. Things that are the same should be very much the same and things that are different should be extremely different. For example, database primary keys should follow exactly one naming convention.

Outline Simple Conventions and Guidelines

Often, *what* the conventions are or *how* you decide to do something don't matter nearly as much as having *decided* on them. Here are some common examples:

- Where source code files should live

- The build tool

- Testing framework

- The HTML templating language

- Naming conventions:

  - Primary keys in the database
  - Class names
  - CSS classes
  - URLs
  - Support files and directories

There are probably many more types of decisions like this and the important thing is that they need to be made, not what the decision is. For example, you could have a lively debate about database primary keys. Should the key for the PERSON table be id or person_id? What is *not* up for debate is that keys should be named consistently. Just make a decision on the naming convention, stick to it, and move on.

It's also worth investigating tools that can "enforce" these conventions. For example, Java developers have long trusted *checkstyle* to report on deviations from an established set of style conventions. Different languages and frameworks have different tooling, but if there are tools that would help, setting them in the project early on will make them significantly more useful than trying to fit them in later.

You should also be cognizant of conventions that exist in the company already. In general, you should adopt these standards unless you have a very good reason not to (and in those cases, make sure everyone understands *why*).

Don't Overdo it & Plan for Change

It can be tempting to produce a laundry-list of conventions and guidelines up front. On the other hand, it might seem daunting to have to make *any* up-front decisions. You need to strike a balance that helps keep the application free of technical debt, but that also serves our original goal of allowing developers to start working as soon as possible.

One way to handle this is to look at the first few features that will be built. What does the application need to have in place to allow those features to be coded? Anything that's not directly related to the features themselves is a good candidate for dealing with now.

The advantage of using features as a guide is that you'll be more likely to make the right decision in the context of actual work, as opposed to pondering what is theoretically good or bad. As you build more and more features, you will likely face more and more of these decisions.

You should also understand - and make clear to the team - that these conventions aren't ends unto themselves. These decisions are supposed to make things easier now. Over time, your application will evolve (e.g. due new requirements) and your conventions must evolve with it. Don't be too rigid and be open to changes when they're needed.

Establish a Culture of Consistency

To keep your application's codebase consistent and easy to follow, but without having to decide everything up front, you want to establish a "culture of consistency", which is fancy way of saying that you value consistency and are willing to spend time during development to keep things consistent.

This also means that you don't have to make all the decisions. Each developer should be encouraged to establish a convention when they first face the need to have one.

For example, you might not know if you need to use database triggers in your application. Therefore, it makes no sense to decide up-front what the naming convention of these triggers should be. However, the first time you *do* need one, spend the small amount of extra time needed to establish a convention about it.

Finally, it's worth considering the political impact of these sorts of decisions. Since it often doesn't matter *what* the decision is, making an unpopular decision can be little gain for a lot of trouble.

For example, at my current job, the team is using the RSpec testing framework for writing automated tests of our Ruby code. I personally prefer Ruby's built-in `Test::Unit` framework that comes with Ruby however, when creating a new application, I stuck with RSpec. The testing framework really doesn't matter, and it ended up being easier to "go with the flow" than have to discuss, and document, my deviation from the de-facto standard.

Consider an Opinionated Framework

Ruby on Rails introduced many developers to the concepts of "convention over configuration" and "opinionated frameworks". The idea seems simple now, but was revolutionary at the time. Instead of allowing ultimate flexibility for developers to decide whatever conventions they'd like to use, an opinionated framework would come with many of these decisions "pre-decided".

For example, in a Rails app:

- All database tables have a primary key field named `ID`.

- The url named `/shipments` will be handled by a piece of code called `ShipmentsController`.

- The class `Purchase` will have fields based on the columns of the database table `PURCHASES`.

There are many more such conventions "baked-in" to the framework. Since Rails' arrival, many frameworks have followed its lead. The result is that there are many frameworks for many languages designed to "just work", as long as you stick to their conventions.

This means that a team using such technologies can get started building features much sooner than a team using a very flexible, un-opinionated technology, simply because they can skip a lot of up-front decision making and start delivering features. Ignore this at your peril.

Roadblocks

Development just starts.

It's possible that, given the technology choice and a list of prioritized features, the team might just start coding. This can lead to massive inconsistencies in the application if you aren't careful. You can deal with this by doing two things:

- Involve the team directly. Look for implicit conventions among the work being produced and ask the developers if they think those conventions should be codified. Often, developers will be happy to have a big impact on the project, and this is an easy way to involve them in these larger decisions.

- Decide quickly. The sooner you decide and can get going, the better. It shouldn't take you longer than a couple days to sort out the basics of the application's architecture. Any development work done during that time can be changed easily to meet with the conventions you come up with.

Resistance to even having conventions.

In some organizations, there is often resistance to the mere notion of a convention or standard. Some developers feel that such standards constrain what they believe to be a creative process.

In a certain sense, this is correct. Overly strict coding guidelines and excessive rules can be more trouble than they are worth. On the other hand, some level of consistency is a good thing.

You can address pushback in two ways:

- Re-examine the established conventions and decisions. Any decision that really doesn't *need* to be made can be deferred. For example, if you don't need to create background processing jobs right now, there's no sense in making a decision about where the source code lives

- Explain the value of the consistency brought about by conventions. Your job is to get the application to a point where everyone can start contributing. By making decisions that allow developers to focus on features instead of infrastructure, the team is more productive.

8.6 Create a Deployment Checklist

Getting your application running in production - the act of deploying it - is usually more complex than simply handing off the source code to an administrator. Your application will likely need to integrate with various internal applications as well as third-party services.

Further, there are aspects of building your application that are orthogonal to its features but are nonetheless important, such as security and monitoring. All of these things amount to a laundry list of unrelated tasks you'll have to do before deploying your app.

What you need to do is find out what should be on this list and create a checklist to make sure you address everything before you first deploy.

Hopefully, your fellow developers and system administrators have such a list, or can help you. If not, you'll need to talk to them yourself to find out what issues you need to be aware of. Here's a generic list to get you started:

- Access to the production database

- Logging and log aggregation

- Authentication/Authorization

- URL or other locator for your app in production

- Analytics

- Crontabs or offline scheduled tasks

- Health check monitoring

- Security scans

- Versions - operating system, programming language, system software

This is just a sample; your situation could be different. Keep in mind that the more you know about these issues ahead of time, the easier it will be to address in your application (especially if you encounter the unexpected).

I was once developing a Ruby on Rails application and planned to use Ruby 1.9.3. Before writing too much code, I started on my deployment checklist. I quickly discovered that the operating system on which I was to deploy didn't have a good build of Ruby 1.9.3 and I would have to use Ruby 1.8.7 instead.

This was not a major change for me at the time, because so little code had been written. Had I not discovered this until the project was underway, it would've been very difficult - if not impossible - to downgrade the version of Ruby I was using.

Once you've got a solid checklist, the ideal next step is to deploy a basic application that addresses everything on the list. I call this a *minimum deployable system.*

8.7 Create a Minimum Deployable System

The items on your deployment checklist represent everything your application has to do to get into the production environment. These typically have nothing to do with user features, but are nonetheless important. As such, the earlier you can address them, the better. The only way to truly address them is to actually deploy your application to production.

By "deploy" I don't mean "make available to users". You'll want to password-protect or hide the initially-deployed application. I like to think of *deployment* as the physical act of getting the code up in the production environment and *launching* as the act of allowing users access.

To make it as simple as possible to be sure you've addressed everything on your deployment checklist, the application you deploy should be as basic as possible. It should have no significant features, and likely do nothing more than pull data from the database, log some messages, and respond to a health check (or whatever else you need to validate the production configuration).

I call this a *minimum deployable system,* because it represents that absolute minimum amount of code and configuration to get the application running in production. This allows you to validate deployment is working without the complication of user features getting in the way.

A secondary goal to deploying your minimum deployable system is to fully automate deployment. Deployment can be a tricky process and the fewer manual steps you have to carry out, the better. Ideally, you run one command which deploys the application.

Hopefully, your organization has such a system in place already, but if not, it will definitely be worth your time to automate whatever steps exist.

Once you get deployment working and can see your app in production, take whatever steps you need to validate that your configurations are correct. This might require access to the application's log or database. You could also set up certain special URLs or screens to validate that the app has been successfully deployed.

Roadblocks

Deployment is a manual process.

Many organizations don't have an easy way to deploy new applications. In this case, the system administrators tend to be so overworked with executing manual instructions that automating things is seen as a luxury, and seldom prioritized.

If there is a shared "QA" environment, or other set of servers where in-development software can be deployed, you might be able to get automated deploys to that server. If the system administrators will allow you access to setup and deploy there, you can use this as an opportunity to automate your app's deployment.

You've never automated via command-line scripts before.

Many developers go years without having to automate things like this. Some developers actively avoid all system administration tasks. This makes some amount of sense; developers are paid to write software, not manage servers. However, only you know your application and how it should behave on production. You are the best person to make sure it gets deployed properly and that everything is working. Also, being able to do enough system programming to deploy an application is a very useful skill.

The more you can understand how systems get deployed, and what each step requires, the easier time you will have working with the system administrator responsible for actually maintaining your application. This skill will also help you at times when there is no system administrator.

So, grab your favorite scripting language and hop to it. You'll be a better developer for it and you will have a much easier time working with your operations team.

Developers are not allowed to deploy.

Some organizations have automated deploys, but do not allow developers to execute them. Often, there is a change management process geared toward a separation of responsibilities between developers and system administrators. You will be unlikely to change this, but you should still try to involve the administrators early. Ask to have one assigned to your team to get the app deployable, even if it won't be "live".

If there is one available, they should be more than happy to solve the deployment challenges earlier rather than later.

Deployment fails repeatedly.

If you are using new technology and are unable to get it deployed, this may indicate that you made the wrong choice of technology. If you are absolutely blocked, you may need to reverse your decision, and go with a more known and conservative approach.

This is unfortunate and even if it's due to you or your administrator's lack of experience, this is the reality you are facing.

The team you have assembled won't be able to deploy the system as designed. It's painful, but it's better than finding out months later after you've built features.

Developers start building features.

With a large or important project, the team will feel pressure to start building features. Although building and deploying a minimum deployable system won't take a lot of effort, it could take a lot of calendar time. You can't expect the team to sit on their hands.

In this situation, either you or the rest of the team should work on a branch in your version control system. You can both do parallel development: you getting deployment working while the rest of the team starts to add features. When your job is done, simply merge the two branches together.

8.8 Add and Deploy Features

At this point, your app is ready to go. You are ready to have developers start building features. Each feature should be built according to the process outlined in the chapter 4. Although you cannot ensure that everyone is working test-first, you should make sure that all features have good test coverage as outlined in that chapter.

Tests are only one way to ensure that the application is working. You also need to see it working after it's been deployed. The best way to do this is to deploy the application after every feature is complete. Since you have the ability to deploy your application with a single step, this should be a snap.

Even if no one but your team can access the app, get each feature into the production (or production-like) environment as soon as it's done, so you make sure it works. This is referred to as *continuous deployment* and is fast becoming a best-practice for software development.

If you have a dedicated QA team, they can do manual testing against this deployed app. I would also recommend that the developer responsible for a feature check it in production. Let them know ahead of time to plan on verifying it in production. This may affect how they build the feature, which is a good thing.

Deploying features as they become available has an additional benefit of being able to show the customer or stakeholder your work-in-progress. You will be amazed at the quality of feedback you get when a user first uses a feature. You want this feedback as soon as possible and by allowing users to really use the features as they are built, you'll get it.

Roadblocks

The corporate culture prevents frequent deployment.

Conservative, slow-moving, or bureaucratic organizations often do not like to involve the customer/stakeholder during development. They often set up projects in a way that makes this difficult, for example by controlling communication between developers and users. Working toward few, large releases is a very "old school" way of thinking - it's how you *had* to release software in the world of physical media. Those constraints don't exist for most modern software projects.

If you've been able to get automated deployment, you can hopefully not worry about this, and just deploy anyway, even if only you and the project manager ever look at the "production" app.

If this isn't possible, perhaps you can do frequent releases to a QA environment. It may be that once management sees the value of viewing running software more frequently, they will be more on board with continuous deployment.

8.9 Moving On

The advice in this chapter is likely going to be the most difficult to follow in this book. While I firmly believe this is the best way to bootstrap an application, very few places I've worked would've made this easy. Fortunately, times are changing and continuous deployment is more widely used than ever.

This part of building a new application can have a large impact on its success, however. The over-arching goal is to allow everyone to focus on building features. Your team shouldn't need to stop building features because of some technical snafu. By taking proper care up front and making the important decisions first, you can keep everyone delivering results.

At this point, you can handle any programming challenge: from small bugfixes to making a new application from scratch. You can make and defend your technical decisions, and can work with others to make business decisions.

In this chapter we got a taste of team leadership, though we'll dive into that more in chapter 12. We'll also talk about how to choose the best candidates for your team in chapter 10.

Before we get to that, there's one more useful skill that you need to pay attention to: writing. Whether it's writing documentation or simply composing emails, your ability to communicate effectively via the written word is crucial. What you write will outlive you and form a lasting impression of who you are. In the next chapter we'll give you a start on making sure that impression is a good one.

9

Learn to Write

Much of this book is about communication, be it through your coding process, technical discussions, or conventions related to a new application. Making sure that others understand your intent is a key aspect of a senior developer. In this chapter, we'll continue this discussion, focusing on the written word.

Almost everything you create as a developer that isn't source code is likely to be written prose. This could be anything from code comments, to emails, to API documentation. Writing is a (more or less) permanent expression of your intent and ideas. It is a way for you to be in many places at once - if a developer can answer his question about your code by reading, rather than finding you, you've accomplished something. Your writing is also a reflection on you as a developer, because it will persist long after you've moved on.

Although writing is fraught with all the same imprecisions, inflections, and tone as any form of communication, with writing you can actually "get it right" before sending it out. It's like code in that way, and this is how we'll approach it.

This chapter will by no means make you the next Thoreau, but my hope is that it can set you on the right course, and give you a few useful tips on improving your written communication

9.1   Three Steps to Better Writing

You can improve your writing immensely by breaking any writing task (even emails) into three simple steps:

1. Get it down

2. Revise it

3. Polish it

Get it Down

Get whatever information you need to impart, whatever argument you intend to make, or whatever email you need to send down "on paper" (likely in your editor or email program). This is analogous to the "fix" step of the "test/fix/refactor" cycle. The idea is to get everything out of your head and into a medium where you can manipulate it more easily.   Don't worry about spelling, grammar, formatting, or anything else. Just get it down.

If you have a large amount of information to write, you may benefit from an outline, and then, for each section, get the information down for that section. Whatever makes it easier for to get started is worth doing. The point of "getting it down" is to reduce all barriers to starting to write. You need words flowing out of your hands as quickly as possible.

Many developers will just stop here, especially with emails. Type it out, click "send", and wait for the replies. As with code, you *might* be able to get away with this and, but chances are you can get better responses and outcomes by actually reading what you've written before calling it "done". You need to revise.

Revise It

Revising is the act of reading what you've written and re-writing some (or all) of it to make it easier to read. It can be difficult (especially for longer texts), and it will be hard to even *remember* to do at first.

Think of this as refactoring your writing. You've gotten down the ideas you need to communicate, but they aren't organized in the best way for someone else to understand.

Unlike when refactoring, revising your writing is going to be more drastic. You may remove a *lot*, and you might rewrite a lot, depending on how much you need to write and how much practice you've had expressing yourself this way. This book, for example, bears little resemblance to what my first draft looked like.

Beyond correcting grammar and spelling mistakes, you want to aim for brevity and specificity. Your writing must focus on delivering results, so the quicker you get to the point, the easier it will be for readers to get the answers they are seeking (or understand what you are asking of them).

Here are a few general guidelines I've found useful:

- Instead of using demonstratives "this" and "that" or pronouns like "it" or "they", use the specific names of things, even if it seems slightly redundant. Technical writing often requires referring to many different things at once, and the reader can become easily confused if you aren't specific.

- Name objects, concepts, and procedures as specifically as you can. Using "thing" should be an absolute last resort. Again, technical writing requires juggling a lot of interconnected nouns in your head, so giving them specific names will make the writing more clear.

- Avoid acronyms, shorthand, or jargon unless you are *absolutely* sure the readers will understand it. Even then, try to avoid it. For longer pieces, create acronyms as needed, but spell them out first. Shorthand and jargon can be impenetrable to many, especially those who aren't working day-to-day with what you're doing. Help the reader by spelling things out or at least by providing a reference to explain jargon.

- Organize thoughts into paragraphs. I've seen *many* developers write in one, giant paragraph, and it makes it very hard to follow. If you go more than a few sentences without a new paragraph, find a way to split it into multiple paragraphs, or consolidate what you have into fewer, shorter sentences.

- Write as if the readers are getting more and more rushed for time as they read. The first sentence should tell them exactly what you want them to do, or what you want them to know.

  Your writing might have many audiences, and they may have wildly different amounts of time to spend reading what you've written. While a developer might need to pour over every detail you've put together, a manager or other decision maker might not have time to read the entire thing. By organizing the "calls to action" up front, you ensure that even the busiest reader will get the point of what you're doing.

Revising, like refactoring, can continue forever if you let it. You need to balance your time against perfecting every last turn of phrase. Often, you can make sufficient improvements by only one pass through your original text. This works great for emails. For longer-lived documents, or more "important" emails, it's worth taking a bit more time. Just be sure to find a stopping point.

When you've formed the words into a readable shape, I like to take a third step to address any aesthetic issues with the text you'll be sending. I call this *polishing* the text.

Polish It

The art of typography is a deep and mystical one, but its purpose is to serve the written word, making it easier to read without altering its meaning. Just as we make our code more readable by indenting it, wrapping long lines, and aligning certain features, formatting our prose in a more pleasant way can make it easier to read.

For our purposes, this means appropriate use of fonts, bold-face, headings, and bullet lists. Technical writing refers to a lot of code, and often contains very specific instructions. You can make vast improvements by the light application of some typography.

Here are some techniques I use frequently, during a final pass through a document before I call it "done":

- Format code in a fixed-width font and/or demarcate it as such. Classes and methods often look like regular English, so setting them off in a code-like font ensures that the reader knows you mean an element of code and not a more abstract concept.

- Use bullet lists or numbered lists liberally. If I have several short paragraphs, or a paragraph of short, explicit instructions or steps, I'll make them into an actual list. This lets the reader know that important points or steps are coming, and allows them to easily locate later.

- Create headings if the document is getting long. If you need to write something that's more than a few paragraphs, headings can help provide signposts and stopping points to guide the reader. Use larger fonts and/or bolder text to indicate a heading.

- If possible, make hyperlinks clickable. If you want someone to follow a link, it's a lot easier for them to click it than to copy and paste it into their browser. It's a small thing, but can help get your message across.

This might all seem superfluous, but polish counts, even if no one realizes you've done it. Taking steps to make your writing easy to read and follow can be the difference between a manager making a snap judgment based on the first sentence of your email and fully understanding what you've written.

If you don't have ready access to rich text formatting in order to make bullet lists, bold text, or headings, I would suggest adopting Markdown, which is a plain text format that accomplishes many of the goals of rich text formatting, but as plain text. Markdown can further be processed into rich text using a variety of tools.

Now that we've covered some basics, let's dig deeper on a few types of writing you're most likely to do as a developer: email, system documentation, and API documentation.

9.2 Write an Email

Most of your writing will be email. Email is the primary form of written communication in any company, and you can be sure that anyone who isn't a developer is spending a significant portion of their day reading and writing email. Typically, the more responsibility you have as a developer, the more you'll be interacting with others, and that means writing more emails.

The worst thing about email, however, is that people don't tend to read their email consistently or completely. It took me many years before I resigned myself to the fact that even though I was diligent in reading my email, most people aren't. I'm not sure why this is, but I have a few guesses:

- An email typically results in the recipient having to do work they otherwise wouldn't have had to do

- Email notifications pop up when email arrives, interrupting other work

- Few people take the time to craft clear and direct messages, making email difficult to read compared to most professionally-written prose, which exacerbates the previous two issues

Whatever the reason, email is a fact of life and is often your only means to communicate with people you need to do your job. Your approach to writing email must take this into account. Most people want to stop reading email as soon as they can, so your job is to get to the point as quickly as possible to allow them to quickly move on, but still provide you the answers you need.

Beyond the "write/revise/polish" cycle we discussed previously, good emails can benefit from a few additional tactics. Here is a list of tips I've found useful in getting response from my emails (this is also a wish list for emails sent to me):

- Ask for only one thing. Many busy professionals, when confronted with a long email, will reply with an answer to the first question they see and hit "Send". Don't ask too many things at once if you can help it.

- Whatever it is you want, write that as the subject in the form of a question. Write your email as if the recipients will read and respond only to the subject line.

- If you need a decision between options, give them short, easy names like "Option A" and "Option B". This makes it easier for recipients to respond, because they don't need to think up (or type) a more complex name that might end up being confusing.

- If you plan to take an action and wish to inform others, or get an "OK", word your email as something you plan to do unless there are objections, e.g. "I'm going to turn off that workaround Monday morning unless anyone has a problem with it". This gives others a chance to weigh in, but alleviates you from having to explicitly get permission as well as removes the burden on the recipient to respond with an "OK".

- Consider having a basic email signature. Many large companies have a corporate-mandated email signature and while it might seem silly, it has its uses. When you first email someone that you don't know, it can be incredibly helpful to them if they know your full name, job title, and other relevant information (such as department or location).

- When forwarding a long email chain to someone for their opinion, don't just write "Thoughts?" and include the entire chain. Summarize what's being discussed and what you'd like from them, instead.

- For a point-by-point response to a long email or email chain, color and bold your response in-line with the original email. It may seem garish, but it'll be a *lot* easier for the recipients to read your responses if they are in, for example, bold, green letters. Just start the email off with "my response are below in green", write your response and go back and color them during the "polish" step.

All of these steps are geared toward quickly getting to the point, and dealing with the fact that busy people don't read their email carefully. System documentation, on the other hand, is often read *very* carefully, because it tends to be a developer's first point of contact with a new piece of code. Let's talk about that next.

9.3 Write System/Application Documentation

Developer documentation for systems, libraries, or applications serves several purposes. In its most basic form, it instructs other developers how to set up and use the code in question. Depending on what the code is it might have more details on getting started, pointers to API documentation, or troubleshooting guides.

The simplest way to document a system, application, or code library is to provide everything in a "README" file at the root of your project. The README is a time-honored place to put such documentation. Tools like GitHub will even render it in HTML.

Unless you have a reason to use another format, use Markdown, which will ensure that your README looks good as plain text, but could be rendered as HTML easily.

Structure your README like so:

1. Intro - summarizes the software for quick reference

2. Overview - detailed explanation of what the code does and why

3. Setup Instructions

4. Other References

Intro

The first line of your README should sum up what the application or system does:

```
# accounts - allow logins from any application
```

Next, you should document how to install the software. Be as clear and explicit as you can, ideally providing copy-and-paste-able information or a link to download the software itself.

For example, if your code is a Ruby Gem, you would do something like this:

```
To install via Bundler

    gem my_gem

or, manually:

    $ gem install my_gem
```

Java-based projects usually provide the relevant XML for Maven:

```
To install via Maven, add this to your pom.xml

    <dependency>
      <groupId>junit</groupId>
      <artifactId>junit</artifactId>
      <version>3.8.1</version>
      <scope>test</scope>
    </dependency>
```

The idea is to allow developers to understand what your code does and give them instructions to start running it as quickly as possible. Anything else related to setup, use, or configuration is handled later.

Overview

Here, you provide more details about what the software does and why it needs to exist. For complex systems or esoteric libraries, it can be hard to sum up in one line, so this is your chance to explain more.

You want this to focus on *why the software exists at all*. What problem does it solve? Why is the solution provided any good? What problems does it *not* solve?

Even if it's just one paragraph of explanation, it can have a huge effect on how your software is perceived and used.

If the software is a code library, include a basic snippet of what the API looks like, to give readers a feel for how they might use the code. For example:

```
The rest-api-client gem provides a very simple
interface for making REST calls:

    RestApiClient.configure(
        :endpoint => example.com/api,
        :version => :v3,
        :token => "<< your api key >>")

    RestApiClient.get("/people/45")
    # => returns a Hashie of the results
```

Setup Instructions

Next, you should provide a *detailed* list of setup instructions. This should be in the form of a numbered list, and each step should, ideally, be copy & paste-able commands that the

135

user can execute. If that's not possible, be as specific as you can about what they need to do.

If possible, provide a way for the developer to validate that they've set up the software correctly. This could be a command to run, a URL to navigate to, or some other action that allows them to test their setup.

If the setup instructions are long and detailed, try to break them down into sections, and give the developer an overview of the sections before they start. Mindlessly executing several dozen command-line tasks can lead to distraction and mistakes. An overview provides some context on what they are trying to accomplish.

At a previous job where I worked, the initial developer setup was quite long, but, if you followed it exactly, it would work reliably. Still, it could become easy to get lost, so we added a section at the start that told the developers what they were doing at a high level:

1. Get access to version control and other systems

2. Check out a copy of the code

3. Compile, test, and run the code

4. Validate access to other systems

Other References

Finally, you want to provide links to other information, such as:

- API Documentation

- Contact info for questions/support/issues

- More detailed documentation if it's available

- Documentation for developing the software, as opposed to using it

A README shouldn't take too long to write, but it's a huge benefit to any developer trying to use your software. On some occasions, you will have a lot more documentation to provide, and doing so in one file can be difficult.

Multiple Files

Some software is complex enough that you cannot fully document it in a README. Your README should still follow the guidelines above, but for additional documentation, provide a link to a web-based system where you can organize the detailed documentation into sections. A wiki is a great way to do this, especially since it allows others to offer corrections or fix documentation errors.

If you cannot put your documentation in such a system, create a `doc` directory inside your project's root directory and provide a series of Markdown files in there. You can use a number-based naming scheme to keep them organized, e.g. `1_Intro.md`, `2_SystemA.md`, etc.

The last bit of writing we'll talk about is API documentation. It's not often that you'll need to write detailed, formal, API docs, but if you do end up having to do this, getting it right and making good reference documentation will help your users as well as yourself.

9.4   Write API Documentation

API documentation is documentation for how to use the publicly exposed bits of code that other developers might need. While it's generally good practice to write some form of API documentation for every public method or function, if your API is going to be widely used, there is a higher bar you will need hit to make the documentation effective.

137

The way I like to approach this is to assume that the reader won't have easy access to the source code. What does the reader need to know to properly use the software in this case? What behaviors of the software might be surprising to someone new? What aspects of the code might be hard to remember, even for experienced users?

An API can usually be documented at two levels: the module and the function. Modules group functions together, and allow the user to go from generic to specific on their quest for the function they need to solve their problem at hand.

A developer might first identify the module that holds the functionality they are looking for and skim that module's documentation. If they find the function they need, they'll navigate down to that function's documentation.

Documenting Modules

What a module is depends on the programming language and system. In the OO world, a module is likely a *class*, although a *package* in Java is a module that contains other modules (classes and more packages). In C, a module is usually defined by functions in a header file.

A module's documentation needs to do three things:

- Easily explain what types of functions it contains

- Provide pointers to commonly used functions or some other starting point

- Show example or idiomatic usage of the module's common functions

Hopefully, you can do this in source code comments that can be extracted and formatted for viewing, such as Javadoc. In that case, follow the conventions of your system as to how to lay out the documentation.

Typically, the first line of your documentation should explain what the module does. For example:

```
/**
 * Formats peoples names according to various
 * locales and other rules.
 *
 * ...
 */
public class NameFormatter {
    // ...
}
```

The remainder of the first paragraph should expand on this *if necessary*. Be concise. If you can sum it up in one sentence, that's fine, end the first paragraph there.

After that, fill in the documentation as needed to describe common usage patterns, along with links to functions and other relevant documentation. This is a roadmap of the module to help users find the right function for their problem.

Continuing our example, we'll document our NameFormatter class, using Javadoc's linking features (the @link directive) to give readers of the generated documentation the ability to click through the function's documentation.

```
/**
 * Formats peoples names according to various
 * locales and other rules.
 *
 * This is the central place for formatting
 * names, as opposed to putting this in the
 * UI layer, and allows consistent formatting
 * in both the UI and in emails.
 *
```

```
 * In most cases, use the no-arg constructor
 * and call { @link #formatFullName(Person) }.
 * See the other constructors for ways to
 * customize the behavior of this class.
 */
public class NameFormatter {
    // ...
}
```

With this roadmap in place, you'll need to document the module's functions.

Documenting Functions

When documenting a function, your goal is to explain to the user what it does, what its arguments mean, and what its possible return values are.

The first line of the documentation should summarize the purpose of the function, allowing anyone to quickly determine if the function is the one they are looking for.

If required, expand on the function's general behavior and reason for being. You want to offer guidance to the user as to when this function should (and should not) be called.

If the function takes arguments, document each one of them in the same manner. The first line should indicate the type expected, and the purpose the argument plays in the function's operation.

Also be sure to indicate if the argument can be null and, if it can, what null means. There's nothing worse than getting an exception from code that should never have been given null in the first place. The same advice goes for optional arguments - document what happens if the argument is omitted.

Document the return value in the same way, especially with regard to the type being returned and if it can be null.

If the function is complex, or has many possible ways of being called (e.g. there are default arguments in play), document some examples and explain what they do.

Here's an example of a complex Ruby method:

```
# Formats a persons name for a web page.
# Instead of string-building in your web views,
# prefer this method, which is feature-filled to
# address any formatting need, while respecting
# locale and internationalization, as well as
# dealing with all the various name formats of
# users in the system
#
# person:: a Person instance whose name is to
#          be formatted
# options:: a hash of options to control the
#           formatting:
#  :informal:: if true, render the name for
#              informal greetings
#              (default false)
#  :sortable:: if true, render the name in a
#              format suitable for sorting.
#              American names, for example,
#              are sortable via "last, first"
#              (default false)
#  :force_locale:: if set, overrides the
#                  detected locale of the
#                  user and uses the
#                  passed-in locale. This
#                  should be a Locale object.
#
# Returns an html_safe string of the users name,
# formatted. Never nil.
#
# Examples:
#
```

```
#     format_name(person)
#     # => Full name, in the order defined
#     #    by their locale
#
#     format_name(person :force_locale => Locale.UK)
#     # => format their name in the UK style always
#
#     format_name(person, :informal => true)
#     # => show only their informal name,
#     #    e.g. first name for Americans
#
def format_name(person,options={})
  # ...
end
```

That's a lot of documentation, but it leaves nothing to doubt. The reader knows **exactly** how the method will work and what can, and cannot, be done with it.

Given all this, however, you may not need to write documentation for every aspect of the method. Assuming your API documentation system can pull out function names, argument names, argument types, and return types, you can omit a fair bit of documentation. For example, consider this Java method:

```
public List<Person> findPeople(Date bornBefore) {
  // ...
}
```

It's fairly obvious what this method does, simply because we have good naming and clear types. I would still add a one-liner like "finds people born before a particular date", so something shows up in the generated documentation, but that would be it. You want your documentation to fill in whatever blanks are missing after the documentation generator has examined your code.

I treat documentation as a "post-refactor" step. When I'm happy with the code, and tests are passing, I'll do one final run through and write documentation as needed. It's also a good time to make sure variable names are consistent and correct. Look for plural/singular agreement, proper spelling, and consistent ordering. Don't forget that your method and parameter names are part of the documentation. Right before you commit is the best time to do it, because the code is fresh in your mind and unlikely to need further changes.

9.5 Practice Writing

Writing is such an important part of being a developer, that you should really cultivate this skill as much as you can. Like any skill, you can improve your abilities with practice. Here are a few ways of practicing your writing:

- Start using Twitter - its short length requirements force you to be brief. You can practice writing for responses by @-replying people more high-profile than you with questions. If you can get a response, it means you've expressed something coherent in just 140 characters.

- Add documentation to open source projects - API documentation on many open source projects is sorely lacking. When you submit changes that enhance the documentation, you are highly likely to get those changes included.

- Write a blog - write short blog entries about your experiences at work or other thoughts on technology. Follow the guidelines we outlined above, and your blog entires will be great.

9.6 Moving On

This chapter is by no means designed to make you an expert technical writer, but it should give you some basic tools and guidelines to help you be effective.

You are now on your way to mastering just about every skill a senior developer needs in order to deliver results. There are only two things left to discuss: building a team, and leading a team. We'll cover building a team first, by talking about technical interviews.

10

Interview Potential Co-Workers

During your time at any given company, new employees will be brought on. You might be involved in this process, helping to vet potential candidates, or you might be in a position to establish a hiring process from scratch.

In either case, your job is to identify developers who can work well with you and your team. You need developers who can deliver results, just like you do. And it's difficult.

In this chapter we'll cover technical interviewing from two perspectives. First, we'll outline what I believe to be an ideal process. I've been on both sides of this process and it's effective and efficient at identifying good developers. After that, we'll talk about other types of technical interviews that are less effective but that you might be required to conduct as part of an existing interview process. We'll see how to get the most out of them.

Note that we'll just be covering the technical interview portion of recruiting, as this is the portion you're likely to be a part of. Discovering candidates, checking references, and other non-technical aspects of the hiring process are outside the scope of this book.

10.1   Ideal Technical Interview

Although each company and candidate are different, you can reliably follow a four step process to determine if a candidate is a good fit:

1. Informal technical discussion to meet and get to know the candidate

2. Have the candidate do a "homework assignment"

3. Conduct a technical phone screen

4. Pair program with the candidate in person.

Although you'll want to conduct each step of this process consistently, you should take into account the role you are looking to fill as well as aspects about the particular candidate in question. We can place these two factors along two axes.

Along one axis is the candidate - how well do you know them? Have you worked with the candidate, and can vouch for them, or is it someone you don't know at all?

The second axis is the organization's need - the role to be filled. How much impact will this person have? Someone in a key position or on a very small team will have a much larger impact than a "rank and file" developer who will be building out features as part of a large, established team. Not everyone needs to (or should) have a huge impact, so it's important to be honest about what you're looking for.

For each step that follows, we'll discuss if it applies to your situation (based on our two-axis approach) and if it does, how to execute that part of the process.

Informal Technical Conversation

This is exactly what it sounds like: a simple, human conversation between two professionals, "geeking out" about technology. The idea is to provide a relaxed environment where you can get a feel for who the person is as a developer. This should not be a harsh "Q&A" looking for esoteric technical knowledge. It should be informal and relaxed, but focused.

You want to make sure to cover the following things in your conversation:

- What your company does and why anyone would work there

- What problems the company has that the candidate might solve

- What the candidate might expect to work on

- The candidates thoughts on technology in general, but also related to what your team uses and what the candidate is familiar with

- Interesting problems the candidate has solved and what excites them about the position

- Any questions the candidate has about the company

For candidates you know, this is crucial. It lets them know that you aren't treating them as just another résumé and that you have respect for them and their work. It's also a good chance to "sell" the candidate on your company without starting a formal interview process.

For candidates you do not know, but who you're hiring in a senior or key position, I would highly recommend this as well, because it's one of the best ways to get a sense of them as a person, including their curiosity, personality, thoughtfulness and higher-level decision-making ability.

For candidates you don't know, but who are being considered for a junior position, this is less important, and can be done as the last half-hour of an in-person interview, possibly with the candidate's prospective manager.

Homework Assignment

Here, you give the candidate a coding assignment that they work on at home over a few days or a week at most. It should be a problem that requires more work than just implementing a function, but not so complex that it requires a huge time commitment. It should also be a problem that has many possible solutions but that you can evaluate easily.

The idea here is to examine the candidate's code, when written in an ideal environment and not under pressure at a whiteboard or on a large screen attached to a laptop.

Be specific about anything you want the candidate to do, but keep in mind that every omitted detail is a chance to learn something about how the candidate thinks. For example, if you fail to document how you'd like the assignment submitted, you might get a `.zip` file, or you might get a link to a GitHub repository, or you might get copy and pasted code. This can be informative.

I would also recommend that you schedule the technical phone screen (discussed in the next section) when you give out the assignment. The candidate is going to spend his or her time writing code for you, for free, and you owe it to them to review it and have a conversation about it. Scheduling the phone screen is the best way to do that.

Finally, have a rubric for evaluating the work. It's important that you evaluate every candidate's work fairly and equally, which can be tricky for subjective attributes such as code quality. A rubric makes sure you check everything and don't over or under-weigh aspects of the solution.

For candidates you do not know, this is a crucial vetting technique for any level. Candidates for senior or key positions should handle this assignment easily. Other candidates should produce quality results and can use it as a chance to shine.

For candidates you already know, this might be something you can skip. Candidates know that homework assignments are for vetting and "weeding out", so giving one to someone whose abilities you are already familiar with can be seen as insulting. This could work against you by preventing strong candidates from continuing through the hiring process.

If you must give these assignments to everyone (it is often a legal requirement to be consistent in all candidate evaluations, depending on where you live), make sure to let the candidate know that, while you are sure of their abilities, your company requires everyone to do these assignments; it's nothing personal. Of course, grade them fairly. On occasion, someone will disappoint you and it's better to find out now.

Technical Phone Screen

The technical phone screen is crucial for candidates you do not know. It's called a "screen" because the idea is to "screen out" candidates who will be unlikely to pass an in-person interview. Bringing a candidate in for a face-to-face interview is expensive and time consuming. The technical phone screen ensures that you keep those expenses to a minimum and don't waste anyone's time by bringing in someone who is unlikely to be a good fit.

A candidate you know and who is interested should be fast-tracked to an in-person interview if possible. In this case, a phone screen could be a barrier to hiring. If your company insists that everyone follow the same process (again, this could be for legitimate legal reasons), make sure to let the candidate know that it's your company's hiring policy and not a reflection on your respect for their skills. To be fair however, have another developer conduct the phone screen.

In any case, once you get the candidate on the phone, tell them your name, your position or title, what you work on (if it would make sense to them), and then outline the structure of the interview:

- Technical questions

- Discussion of the homework

- Questions the candidate has for you

Technical Questions

Steve Yegge has an excellent post about technical questions to ask during a phone screen. I've used his technique on many phone screens and find it effective at identifying candidates who are knowledgeable.

He asks five questions that cover a wide range of computer science, each designed to test for what he feels is basic knowledge any programmer should have:

- Write some code for a simple problem

- Talk about software design

- Demonstrate knowledge of scripting languages

- Demonstrate knowledge of data structures

- Demonstrate basic understanding of bit manipulation

These might not make sense for your or your company, but pay attention to how they are organized. These five types of questions cover a very broad range of programming knowledge, from high level design, to low level bytes, to pragmatic use of scripting languages. Design your phone screen questions similarly and always use the same ones each time. If you find candidate are passing your phone screen but failing the in-person part of the interview, ask more difficult questions in the phone screen for future candidates.

As you talk, be sure to write down the candidate's answers. Don't just check "got it" or "missed it". Describe what their answers were. The reason for this is that if a candidate does well but doesn't nail the in-person interview, your notes from the phone screen might help make a final decision.

Discussion of the Homework

The candidate spent time on the homework assignment and deserves to have it reviewed by a developer. Discussing code is also a great way to get a feel for how the developer thinks and approaches a problem. If you haven't already reviewed the candidate's homework (I recommend the reviewer and phone screener be the same person), do so before the interview.

You should have a list of questions and comments about the code, but first get the candidate talking about the assignment. What was their approach? Was it easy? Challenging? Confusing?

Once the candidate has given you their overview of the assignment, go through your list of questions and comments. Be sure to praise anything you liked about their solution. This will make discussing negatives easier, but will also demonstrate that you value good work and will openly praise it (a selling point for you and your company).

Keep it casual and avoid any divisive arguments. Your goal

is to understand how the candidate thinks when solving a problem, not to prove that your particular solution is the best.

Questions the Candidate has for You

When you've got what you need, it's important to let the candidate ask questions of you. The candidate will certainly be curious about the company and you can use this time to "sell" them on it.

Be sure to be honest with your answers. If you are asked about something that wouldn't put the company in a good light, be honest, but put a positive spin on it.

I worked a job once with almost 100 applications in production. One of the older applications had a very challenging codebase that everyone ended up having to work with for various reasons. When a candidate asked me about, I was honest: the codebase is not fun to work with. But, I turned it into a positive: management knew about the problems and was in full support of the team porting or refactoring the problem areas.

Once you've answered all the candidate's questions (or the time is up), thank them for their time, and let them know that they'll hear from someone one way or the other. If they did exceptionally well, and you're sure you'd like to meet in person, definitely let them know. If, on the other hand, they did poorly and are unlikely to be called in for an in-person interview, keep that to yourself and discuss it with your hiring manager, recruiter, or simply sleep on it.

Pair Programming

When a candidate comes in for an in-person interview, or otherwise has passed the phone screen, you should be confident that the candidate can code and can work on the team. The last step is to find out for sure.

The best way to find out if the candidate can really code and really be a part of your team is to pair program with them. You should do this for every candidate, regardless of position or previous experience.

In a normal pair programming scenario, the two developers equally divide their time between typing code and watching the typer. For the interview, I would let the candidate do most of the typing. This will be most comfortable for someone not used to pair programming, but is also a good way for you to evaluate them, since your head won't be in coding, but in observing them navigate the problem. I'd recommend you have them bring their personal development laptop to the interview.

As to the problem to work on, it depends on several factors. If you are a small startup, or are hiring someone in a key position, I would recommend spending over an hour on a real problem (or as real as you are comfortable with). Working on a legitimate problem you yourself might have to solve will be the best way to see how the candidate performs.

For larger teams, or for hiring more junior developers, I'd recommend using a simpler problem that can be solved in about 30 minutes, and use the same problem for everyone.

In either case, you want to allow the candidate to do whatever they need to in order to keep working. Allow them to search the Internet, ask questions, look things up, or do anything else they'd be able to do if they really worked with you. This is a real-world simulation.

If the candidate gets stuck, give hints as necessary to keep them working. It's better to get the candidate to a solution with help than let them struggle and use up all their time.

At the end of the programming session, you should have a good feel as to how this person works, and if they would be a good fit for the team.

Many companies use a wide variety of other interview types (which we'll cover in the next section) but in my experience, actually coding with someone is the only way to be sure. The only better way would be to hire then for a one to two week project, but this is often infeasible.

Once you've taken the candidate through this process, your next job is to make a decision: do you extend them an offer?

Making a Decision

Once you've completed the interview process, you'll need to make a hiring decision. If you did the entire interview by yourself, it's easy: decide based on what you experienced. It's more likely that you weren't the only one involved. This means that everyone who *did* participate has some vested interest in the decision.

It's also important that whoever will be assembling that offer (which will include salary and other compensation) has a strong understanding of the strengths and weaknesses of the candidate. To this end, I would recommend that everyone involved in the interview meet as soon after the candidate is done as possible and discuss the candidate's performance.

Let everyone get comfortable talking about the candidate and weighing in on how they performed. Make sure you hear from each person. I'd recommend going around one-by-one and getting verbal feedback.

Next, call for a vote. Everyone should vote either "hire" or "no-hire" and everyone should vote at the same time. An easy way to do this is to count to three and have everyone give a thumbs-up or thumbs-down. Doing it this way prevents "anchoring" where people vote with the majority who might actually have reservations. You need the most honest feedback you can get.

At this point, anyone who voted "hire" should be given the chance to convince anyone who voted "no-hire" to change their vote. Allow for votes to be called for again but, once each person seems content with their vote, make a decision.

I'd recommend you make an offer only if everyone voted "hire". This means you allow anyone to veto the candidate. The reasons are threefold:

- It's possible the "no-hire" is aware of a shortcoming that everyone else isn't, but isn't quite able to explain it. It doesn't mean the shortcoming is invalid.

- It's safer to walk away if you aren't 100%. There is more risk in a bad hire than missing out on a great hire. This is especially true of candidates who will have a large impact.

- The team's morale will start to suffer if their objections are ignored. Disregarding a "no-hire" vote sends a message that the employee's participation in the process provided no value; you would've reached the same outcome had they not participated at all.

This is the ideal interview process. Many organizations have their own process, which interviewers are asked to follow. Even if you can't conduct the ideal process we've outlined here, you can still get a lot of value out more "traditional" interviewing techniques.

10.2 Other Types of Interviews

In this section, we'll go over several common interview techniques and discuss how you can get the most out of them. None of them are as efficient as a homework assignment and pair programming but, in combination, they can be effective.

As we'll see, each technique offers an incomplete picture of the candidate, so you must combine many of these techniques to decide if a candidate should be given an offer.

155

This means that in-person interviews are time and labor intensive.

Here are the techniques we'll discuss:

- Code a solution to a simple problem

- Outline the code to a more complex problem

- Outline the design to a large problem

- Technical Q&A

- Brainteasers

- Non-technical problem solving

Code a Solution to a Simple Problem

Here, you present the candidate with a basic problem and ask them to code the solution, looking for an exact answer (i.e. not pseudo-code). The FizzBuzz test is a classic example of this interviewing technique. The idea here is to see if the developer - without any other resources but their own wits - can actually translate a problem into code.

FizzBuzz is the perfect type of question for this technique, because any competent programmer can solve it in a few minutes, and it weeds out anyone who just can't code at all. It's possible that it's well-known enough that some candidates can just memorize it, so you may need your own problem here.

Whatever you come up with, it should be incredibly simple to explain and understand. The solution should require some sort of iteration, one or two basic comparisons/expressions, and have a solution that "fits" on one screen or on one whiteboard.

You should personally be able to solve this instantly and you should also be able to recognized valid alternatives. I would recommend keeping a set of test data with you and running through that with the candidate when they think they've got the solution.

Often, candidates are asked to solve this on a whiteboard or piece of paper. One advantage of this is that developers are often required to explain something or show code on a whiteboard, e.g. in a meeting. The main disadvantage of this is that, well, programmers don't write code by hand on a whiteboard.

If you can, provide a computer, or allow the candidate to use theirs, and watch the screen (or hook it up to a projector). This isn't pair programming, but the candidate will be far more comfortable and you'll be judging them based on a closer approximation of actually programming.

You should prepare some follow-up questions or "extra credit" if the candidate gets the answer very quickly. For example, you could have the candidate improve the performance of their solution, or re-write it recursively, or some other small tweak. This will allow you to get even more insight into the candidate and also make sure they really understand their solution.

This interview technique will only tell if the candidate possesses the most basic coding skills. This is useful as a first interview to weed out candidates that simply cannot code, but it should be no means be the only code related interview.

Outline the Code to a More Complex Problem

This is a variation on the previous task of coding a simple solution on a whiteboard or computer. Here, you present the candidate with a more complex problem, and ask them to sketch out a solution. You aren't looking for working code here and pseudo code is probably OK.

The idea here is to focus on the candidate's problem-solving abilities rather than the specifics of writing working code.

The reason for this is pragmatic: you likely don't have the time to fully solve a more complex problem, but you need a way to measure the candidate's low-level design and problem-solving skills.

The types of problems you want to give here should be ones that you can personally provide a very quick solution to, even at a code level, but that could have various legitimate solutions. You should also have an easy way to judge the correctness of the candidate's approach, e.g. with a rubric.

Ideally, the problem also can lead to interesting discussions and follow-on questions, to really probe how the candidate thinks. This could be in the form of changing requirements or discussing the performance aspects of the solution.

An example I have used is to have the candidate implement an immutable stack data structure. Typical solutions involve copying a lot of data to keep the stacks immutable, which is inefficient and can lead to discussions of performance and complexity. Further, the very nature of the problem is a good jumping off point for discussing concurrency.

Assuming the candidate went through the previous interview technique as well, this can give you a decent picture of the candidate's abilities to implement small features or bugfixes.

Outline the design to a large problem

Here, we present a much larger problem, and have the candidate outline a basic design or approach to solving it. This tests the candidate's ability to handle complex problems that can't be addressed simply by coding.

The ideal problem is one with no particular solution and that requires various design tradeoffs. As the interviewer, you should be familiar with the problem domain and be able to easily produce a solution, so that you can more easily evaluate the candidate's responses.

The structure of this exercise will be more conversational, simply because you can't get into specifics. It's a good idea to tell the candidate this beforehand, so they don't end up struggling on minutiae. With this context, you should interrupt them frequently to talk about what their doing and why. Don't be afraid to take side trips to see what the candidate knows.

Good problems here are to design a system for a domain the candidate might be familiar with. The game Monopoly, for instance, is well known to many, and has some nuances to it that make it interesting. Designing a web server or application server might also work. You need to make sure the candidate understands the domain already (you don't want to have them learn a new domain while also designing a solution for it). Have several problems ready and pick the one that requires the least "ramp up" from the candidate.

For Candidates in senior or key positions, this can be a good indicator of their ability to explain ideas and make convincing arguments. Do not rely on this as the sole measurement of technical ability, however. It's very easy to hand-wave through an exercise like this and not be able to produce working code when the time comes.

Technical Q&A

This interview type is more of a "grab bag" of technical knowledge, designed to see if the candidate knows what they are talking about. If a candidate has SQL on their résumé, you'd ask them some SQL questions. If they've used Ruby on Rails, you'd ask some Rails questions.

The idea is to sanity-check the candidate's experience and ability to talk about it. Typical questions here are those that have specific answers, and are related to technologies, tools, or techniques that your team users, or that you have experience with.

This can be a frustrating exercise for the candidate, especially if the questions are chosen around rote memorization and lack any requirement to problem-solve.

To get the most out of this, have questions prepared that require the candidate to solve a problem or explain something in detail. For example, for a junior developer who has SQL on his résumé, I might present a sample schema and ask for some SQL to query various bits of data, with each question I ask requiring more and more SQL knowledge.

This type of interview isn't very effective, because it's fairly easy to pass. You'd have to pretty much lie on your résumé or be the world's worst communicator in order to fail here. In both of those cases, the candidate would do poorly on other more informative interviews, so this is not an effective technique.

Brainteasers

This type of interview involves having the candidate solve abstract problems that have no basis in programming or even reality. The intent is to focus on pure problem-solving and creative thinking.

An example would be an egg-drop: You have two eggs, both of which are identical in every way. You also have access to a 100-story building. Your job is to figure out the highest story from which you can drop an egg and have it not break in the minimum number of drops. Once you drop an egg and it breaks, you obviously cannot use it anymore, but you aren't required to have any eggs left when you're done [1].

There are countless others that you can find, but what they all have in common is that they are haphazard at best in revealing anything about a candidate.

---

[1] If you can't sort out the solution, don't worry. I held an optimal solution in my head for many years only to have one of my tech reviewers point out that I was wrong. Read all about it here

There are two reasons for this:

- The candidate might know the problem's solution from having read about it or being asked about previously. They will get it instantly, and you will have learned nothing about them.

- These problems often require a "moment of inspiration" that might not come, but can be hard to coax out with hints. Candidates who would be productive and creative contributing members of your team might just "not get it" through no fault of their own.

I would avoid these questions entirely or, if you must perform this type of interview, put little stock into the outcome. The only thing you might learn is that the candidate gets frustrated easily and lets it show. Such a candidate will certainly reveal their true colors in other, more useful interviews.

Non-technical Problem Solving

This is a combination of brainteasers and the "design a large system" question from earlier. It's epitomized by the now-famous Microsoft interview questions like "how many piano tuners are there in New York City?"

These problems are designed to focus solely on the candidate's problem-solving abilities and creative thinking. The idea is to give them a problem for which there is no realistic answer and observe the candidate try to sort through it.

Whatever question you give, you should have your own answer, and should be familiar enough with the problem domain to make sure the candidate is considering all aspects of the problem. I would recommend questions focused around actually solving a problem ("how would you move

Mt. Everest") instead of reverse-engineering a design ("why are manhole covers round?").

You should allow them a lot of leeway to hand-wave over specifics. The idea is to remove any constraints about the solution that you can. For example, I was once asked to measure the amount of water that was flowing under the Key Bridge in Washington, DC at any given time. I invented non-existent, but reasonable, technology to do so; how else was I supposed to solve the problem?

One advantage this question has over the "design a large system" question is that it can be conducted by a non-technical person on your team. As with the more technical version, this can be revealing about how a candidate approaches a problem, but this should by no means be considered as any indicator of technical ability.

10.3 Moving On

Hopefully, you will be in a position to determine how you vet developers' technical abilities before hiring them. Nothing beats actually working with someone to determine how good they are and what kind of asset they'll be to your team.

If you are stuck with a mandated process, you can now navigate it more effectively and get the most out of it. They key is to always be prepared, and provide detailed feedback to the hiring manager on what you've observed.

Interviewing candidates is one of the many non-programming related tasks a senior software engineer is expected to complete throughout the work week. It can often seem impossible to balance requests for your time with the need to get features delivered. In the next chapter, we'll see how to do that, by scheduling interruptions as part of the workflows we've already learned about.

11

Be Responsive and Productive

We're nearing the end of our journey and we've discussed a lot of techniques to help you be the best software engineer you can be. The most powerful technique is the ability to do all this amidst the day-to-day distractions of a fast-paced, functional business.

You aren't the only person who has work to do, and delivering working software isn't the only result you're expected to deliver. As a developer, you hold more value than the ability to produce code. You understand the problems you're solving at a detailed level. You understand the ramifications of product decisions, know what's possible, and how much effort difficult solutions can take.

This information is valuable to your team and your organization, and part of your job is to use your specialized skills and knowledge to help others achieve their goals, even if it doesn't require writing code, and even if it means you have to stop what you're doing to do so.

You have to be *responsive*, without sacrificing your productivity.

11.1   Being Responsive to Others

If you keep your head firmly in code, ignoring emails and instant messages for hours on end, you may deliver your software tasks more quickly, but you'll only be providing *part* of the service you're hired to provide. You will not be seen as a leader and rightly so–you'd be focusing all your effort on coding, not leading your team or company to solve challenging problems.

As we'll see in chapter 12, leading a team requires more than just technical skill, but the ability to organize multiple tasks, and to garner the trust and confidence of everyone involved in a project. By eliminating all "distractions" and just focusing on coding, you will not build that trust or engender confidence.

The reason a lot of developers shy away from this is that it's *hard*. Programming is an activity that requires extend periods of concentration, where a 30-second tap on the shoulder can result in 15 minutes of lost productivity. Since **most** of a programmer's time is spent coding, it seems enticing to just cut off all outside communication for the majority of your work day.

A senior developer can't do that. A true technical leader must be available to others while still getting the job of coding completed in a timely fashion.

A common way to do this is to divide responsibilities. The team lead will "absorb" requests for programmer expertise, thus shielding the developers "on the ground" from the distractions. This breaks down at any real scale, however.

As the team lead spends more and more time facing outward, they'll be less and less knowledgeable about the work being done. Taken to an extreme, you have a technical manager who hasn't worked with the code in years and can only be helpful to a point on technical matters. The developers they manage will need to help out.

Further, the more a single person becomes the only point of contact for technical input, the more that person will be in demand, and resourceful product managers, designers, and business folks will "route around" the busy tech lead and talk to the other developers anyway.

What this means for you is that you cannot rely on a team lead or manager to shield you from all distrations. You'll *have* to learn how to get your work done while still providing non-coding help, direction, and advice to the rest of the organization.

When your entire team is able to do this, you'll end up having a great relationship with the rest of the company, which builds trust and confidence, and you'll also continue delivering results as you have been. And when it's your time to lead and make decisions, you'll be known as responsive and productive, which greatly eases the difficult task of building consensus on technical solutions.

The key to making this work is to invert your relationship with your "distractions" like email and instant messenger. Instead of letting them interrupt you, pro-actively schedule time to check them, instead.

11.2   Pro-actively Schedule Interruptions

There is research to support this approach. In Fogarty:05, researchers found that programmers had the hardest time resuming their work when interrupted during editing or reading code, which should hardly be surprising. Interestingly, in Trafto:03, researchers found that if a programmer can plan for an interruption, that programmer will resume their task much more quickly after the interruption is complete.

What this means that if you can work toward a "good breaking point" frequently, you can actually stop at those breaking points and pro-actively check-in with your normal sources of interruption. Instead of having your email and instant messenger grab your attention at an inopportune time, you invert the relationship by "polling" at a time of your choosing, for example, when you've finished refactoring a bit of code you just wrote.

The key, then, is to ensure you structure your work such that it affords many good breaking points, and to create a reasonable schedule for checking email, instant messages and the like. If you've been following the advice in this book, your work is generally structured around the process described in chapter 4. This process affords many good breaking points, because we use code, in the form of tests, as a means to store our current context.

Figure 11.1 shows a detailed view and how each of those steps can afford a planned interruption. You'll note that during times where we're thinking and writing code, either writing a test or making a test pass, we can't afford an interruption. But, once we've gotten to a known state, either a failing test, a passing test, or a successful refactor, we have enough context in our tests and code that we can stop and check email or instant messenger.

You'll also note that when we're either about to write an acceptance test, or one has just successfully passed, we can suffer a longer interruption, since we've completed a larger chunk of work.

What's interesting to think about here is that if you *don't* drive your development by tests, and *don't* work outside-in (by driving features with acceptance tests), you will not suffer interruptions very well, and will either work more slowly as you deal with requests for your time, or become unre-

Figure 11.1: Scheduling Interruptions

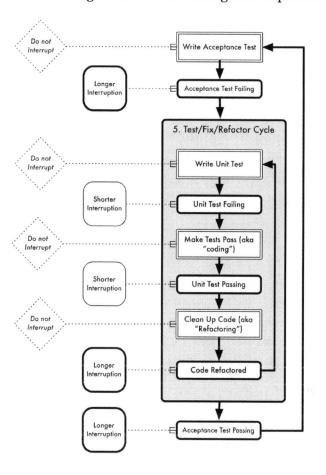

sponsive as you block-off the outside world in an attempt to maintain your context.

Now that we can see *where* in our process we can afford to look up and check to see if we're needed by others, we have to make sure that in doing so, we respond appropriately without losing any context not captured by our tests. To do that, we're going to establish a personal service-level agreement (SLA) regarding various forms of communication.

11.3   A Personal SLA for Communication

Given that we need to be responsive, even while coding, and that we're going to do that by pro-actively checking for interruptions when we are in a good place, the question is how to do that without spending our entire day reading and writing email or chatting on instant messenger. We must strike a balance between responding to requests for our time and actually getting programming work done. The key is a personal service-level agreement.

We want others to know that they can get requests in front of us and that we'll respond to all requests, including timely responses to urgent issues. Ideally, we want all of this coming through email, with instant messages (and physical interruptions) reserved only for urgent needs.

We have to strike a good balance with our SLA, because the less responsive we are to email we are, the more instant messages we're going to get as people can't be sure we're getting their requests. The more instant messages we ignore, the more likely it is someone is going to come over and interrupt us at an inopportune time.

Instead of discussing an SLA in an abstract sense, I'll outline my personal SLA to give you a sense of how it might work. You can adjust this as needed. Note that I don't explicitly advertise this SLA to others, but I follow it consistently. The result is that I am rarely interrupted by instant messages or the phone, because I can be relied-upon to respond to requests in an appropriately timely fashion.

Managing Email

The key to making this work is to route requests through email and to manage your email effectively. Effective email management requires separating *reading* email from *responding* to email, as well as a small bit of organization around your inbox.

Essentially, your inbox should represent emails you need to read or respond to. Unread messages require a reading, read messages require a response. It's that simple.

When you've responded to an email, move it to another folder (i.e. archive it, do not delete it). If your email client isn't good at search, you may need to better organize your archive, or transfer information to a better format, but make sure you can find emails later if you need to.

Given this, here's my SLA for emails (outlined in figure 11.2):

- All email read once per hour during normal business hours. *Read*, not responded to. Because I'm checking every hour, this "audit" is usually very quick and doesn't require a massive context switch. I call this an "hourly audit", but it happens any time I can suffer a longer break in my workflow.

- Urgent emails (by my assessment of urgency) get a response within an hour, typically during the hourly audit. In other words, as I read, I make an assessment of the request. If it seems genuinely urgent (which is not just "urgent to me", but appears urgent to the team or company in general), I'll respond then. If it's not urgent, I move onto the next email.

- All emails requiring a response get a response by the next business day. All of them. Typically this means either at the end of the day requested or the start of the day after the request, as those are both good times to delve deeper into email.

- If I cannot provide the requested information in one business day, I'll respond with an estimate of when I can, and then schedule time to find the information.

- All information requested is provided within five business days. Five days gives me ample time to schedule a few hours of research without disrupting my current programming priorities.

Figure 11.2: Managing Email

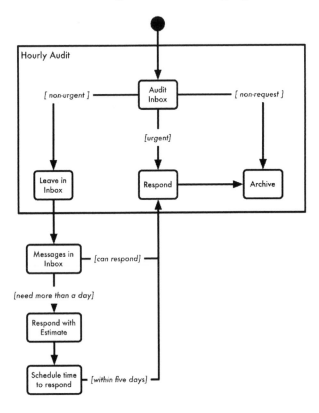

Because of the hourly audit, and the response-within-a-day, anyone has a reliable avenue to get information in front of me. Urgent requests will get read within an hour and responded to do then, but responding to non-urgent requests don't need to interrupt me.

Because I'm controlling when these messages take my concentration, it's easier to fit them into my workflow. It doesn't take a lot of brainpower to scan an email to see if it needs a response. Usually, no emails require such a response, so I can flip back to my editor and see what test is failing.

This also means that actual interruptions are kept to a minimum. Because I'm generally responsive throughout the day, I can more easily defer non-urgent interruptions generated by those who aren't respecting my time. They know they can quickly get a response without coming over to my desk.

Managing Interruptions

Be it instant message or a tap on the shoulder, an interruption is going to be disruptive because you will not have been able to schedule it, and cannot plan for a good stopping point. Dealing with this requires a two-pronged approach: first send reliable signals as to your availability, and second, shunt these interruptions through email whenever possible.

Instant messages are easier to deal with. Primarily, it's because you can let them linger for several minutes before allowing them to grab your attention. As soon as you see your test pass or fail, you can take a quick glance at any IMs that are waiting for you. If you really need to avoid this distraction, you can set your status to away, or simply log out. Use this power sparingly, as it often will only serve to route requests to more disruptive channels.

For physical contact, you want to send a signal that are you in the middle of working. The easiest way to do this is either close the door to your office (if you are lucky enough to have one) or put on headphones (even if you aren't listening to music). It's a subtle signal, but someone looking to "bounce an idea off you" or engage in smalltalk will think twice if you've erected some physical separation. Just be sure to take your headphones off or open your door when you aren't deep in the code. A pattern of both availability and unavailability will make each a more powerful signal.

With those boundaries set up, you next must deal with the

interruptions themselves. If it's not plainly obvious that the requester has an urgent need, simply ask "is this urgent?". Take their word for it, whatever the response. Time spent debating the urgency of their request is better spend just giving them the help they need.

If their request isn't urgent, politely if they can send you the request in email. You can simply explain that you're in the middle of something and will be happy to give their request your full attention later. Because you're diligently managing your inbox, your interrupting co-worker will either already be aware of your responsive nature or will be pleasantly surprised when, true to your word, you get back to them quickly.

11.4   Moving On

The techniques we've described here all serve to create a pattern of responsiveness. This will engender trust, which gives you more control over how you handle non-programming related tasks. Being responsive to other members of your team without sacrificing your productivity is a key ability to being a reliable leader.

And this brings us to the last chapter of the book, which is how to lead a team. Leading a team requires more responsiveness than simply writing code, and by mastering a workflow that includes responding to requests for information, you'll already be a leg-up when it comes time for you to lead team.

12

Lead a Team

It's been a long journey - from small bug fixes, to complex features, to new applications - but almost all of it has focused inward: what do *you* do to excel at being a senior developer? Eventually, you will be less responsible for these sorts of tasks and more responsible for getting a team of developers focused on a common goal. I'm not talking about so-called middle management, where a possibly-technical person organizes programmers but does no actual programming, I'm talking about a technical lead.

Your company may not call this position "technical lead", or it may not be a formal position, but the role I'm describing is essentially being the most all-around senior person on the team.

The technical lead is exactly what it sounds like: a leader in the realm of technology. The tech lead is usually responsible for making technical decisions. The tech lead might be the single point of contact between the team and project stakeholders. Or, the tech lead is simply the most respected member of the team, who holds everyone together and guides them toward a common purpose.

The difference between general managers and tech leads is that tech leads write code. Tech leads must be familiar with the codebase and are often the most familiar. They will typically implement the trickiest or most critical features, since they are the most experienced, or most trusted on the team to do so. They also will have a say in who implements what features or getting estimates for proposed work.

The topic of team leadership and general people management is huge. As such, we aren't going to focus on techniques for general people management. Instead, we'll focus on the challenges specifically faced by a tech lead. These challenges exist regardless of your explicit job requirements or mandates by management. As such, we'll discuss dealing with them in practical way that's, you guessed it, focused on delivering results.

Never forget that this is your goal. Every chapter up to this one dealt with what *you* could do to deliver results *yourself.* As a tech lead, you must find a way to get *others* to deliver those results. This is potentially the most difficult part of transitioning from "line coder" to actual tech lead.

Getting your team to deliver results is going to require that you set aside some of your duties as a programmer. For example, we'll learn about how to effectively review code and, while it's not an onerous process, it *will* take time to do.

Being the team lead means understanding that your participation in non-coding activities is of greater value to the team than your ability to add new features or fix bugs. Don't be too alarmed; even the busiest tech leads spend most of their time coding. You just need to be cognizant of your new role and how best to serve the team. You also need to be organized and efficient with your non-coding activities.

To understand what challenges you'll face and how to deal with them, we'll go through a typical project life cycle from start to finish. At each phase, we'll outline the issues you'll need to deal with as tech lead, and how to approach them.

Your involvement in a project could be in any of the following four phases:

1. Starting the project

2. Delivering the project

3. Enhancing the project and fixing bugs

4. Leaving the project

12.1   Start the Project

Here, a project is being considered, and a team is being formed. You've been chosen to lead the project or to be the first developer to work on it. If you have never lead a project, but are in the situation of being asked to develop something from scratch, this is a great opportunity to demonstrate (or develop) your skills as an effective leader. Even if you are the only developer to work on the project initially, your actions in managing the project will demonstrate your ability to lead.

To get the project started out on the right foot, you'll need to consider the following things:

- The business problem being solved

- The team members

- Delivery schedule

- Delivery process

- Bootstrapping the application

Let's go over each of these.

The Business Problem Being Solved

As ever, you need to know what problem the proposed software is going to solve. You need to be intimately familiar with the areas of the business this project will affect.

Although there might be analysts or subject matter experts available to you, you shouldn't rely on them entirely for domain knowledge about what this new application is supposed to do. Requirements will never be specific enough and you and your team will be the ones filling in the blanks. The more you know, the better you'll be able to do that and the more successful the project, your team, and you will be.

Further, the better you understand the business problem, the more impact you can have on what the application does and how it will work. As the technical lead on the team, you bring expertise that no one else has, namely how technology can solve the problem at hand. Without a deep understanding of the business problem, you won't be effective in this role.

Depending on the domain, it can be tricky to go from zero to complete understanding in a reasonable amount of time. A good proxy for being an actual expert is to identify measurable aspects of the business that this project will affect. For example, your software might enable high efficiency for a data entry task. You can measure that efficiency and track if the software is making the expected improvement.

Once you have a grasp on the problem you're solving, the next step is to form the development team.

The Team Members

It is unlikely that you will get to chose whoever you want to be on your team. Most organizations have a constant need for new developers and you may either be assigned a team based on who is available or - at best - get to choose from some who *are* available.

The initial part of any project is fraught with chaos. Stakeholders want features delivered, you need to establish a technical architecture in which everyone can work, and developers want something to do. In order to make this initial phase as painless as possible, I would strongly suggest trying to limit the size of your team initially, and plan on adding members once the project is underway.

Ideally, you would be the only technical member at first. Working alone leads to incredible efficiency. You don't need to discuss or exchange knowledge with anyone and can simply deliver working code.

The size and scope of your project may make this untenable, but I would still recommend a small team initially: no more than three developers including yourself.

When you do add developers to your team, and you have some ability to choose who to consider, the following factors are good indicators of productive team members.

Recently shipped a successful project Shipping code is the best way to ground yourself in the real world and understand the tradeoffs between slop, technical debt, and clean code. If a developer hasn't shipped anything, or hasn't done so recently, this could be a red flag that they are unable to distinguish the difference, or cannot understand the business purpose of software.

Writes code driven by tests Developers that drive their work via tests will not only deliver higher quality code more quickly, but will be easier for you to work with, since that's how you work. You'll spend less time doing code review and arguing about process and more time delivering value.

Excited or knowledgeable about the technology Regardless of the technology you're going to use, a developer that's excited about it is going to approach work with a more positive and enthusiastic attitude. If the technology is new to you, having an expert on the team can be very handy.

Has significant experience If you have only one other team member, you want it to be someone who has enough experience that they can be relied-upon to complete work without a lot of hand-holding. You want someone who can quickly understand the problem, sketch out an approach and go. The initial stages of a project are not the time for mentoring younger team members who are still learning how to solve problems with code. Such junior members can be an asset later on, but initially, you need someone senior to get the project going.

Ultimately, you want developers that you can rely on to do the right thing, and whose work you will not have to check very often. At the start of the project, the bar for being on your team should be as high as you can make it.

While forming the team, or soon after, you will need to provide some sort of estimate around when the software will be available. Depending on what's expected, this might be a date or might be a series of dates, so we'll think of it as a schedule.

Delivery Schedule

When discussing a new project, the stakeholders will be very interested in when the project will be done. This is when you run the risk of making promises you cannot keep. Everyone has to understand that it is impossible to know with any certainty when the project will be "done".

First, it's unrealistic to have a definition of what the project should do at any level of specificity; you have no definition of "done". Second, without a team or technology choice, even if you *did* know what "done" means, you don't know what you have to work with to get the project delivered.

Nevertheless, the stakeholders deserve some sort of assurance as to when they can start using the software. Despite the massive unknowns in starting a software project, you have to come up with a delivery schedule.

First, identify any hard deadlines. A hard deadline is one that is more or less immutable, based on factors outside the control of the team. A common example is the timing of a feature or product release with a marketing campaign.

What's important to understand is that an arbitrary date chosen by an executive or project manager is *not* a hard deadline (although you should consider the fact that said executive is privy to information you are not; try to find out before dismissing arbitrary dates). That being said, a hard deadline could be a date after which the project is no longer financially feasible. For example, if the project can't be delivered in three months, it'll cost more money than it will save and thus not be worth it.

Next, you need a prioritized list of features. The features should be hard-ordered such that there is exactly one feature with highest priority, one with the second-highest, and so on.

If the hard deadlines relate to features directly (e.g. "we need feature X by July 7th"), those should inform your priorities. Every feature required by a particular date should be prioritized higher than those not required by that date.

Getting stakeholders to agree to this can be difficult. To help them understand why it's important, let them know that you'll be building things in order, and won't have any more features in progress than you have developers, so the features will get prioritized eventually.

You now have a list of features and possibly some dates. If you have no hard deadlines, you've got more flexibility, but the job of estimating is still difficult. You now need to create a delivery schedule that gives the project stakeholders some idea of when and what will be done, but that doesn't hamstring your team into keeping promises that aren't realistic.

Your schedule will be comprised of two parts. First is an estimate of what will be delivered when. This should be as vague or specific as your requirements and I'd recommend discussing it with the team to come up with a ballpark. This is a *huge* topic that would be impossible to cover here and there are many techniques available. Most literature on agile software development can give you some guidance and options (See the reading list in appendix E for few places to start).

The second part of the delivery schedule is a promise: you promise to re-evaluate the schedule on a regular basis, based on work completed, and the stakeholders promise not to hold you to original dates if reality gets in the way.

In agile parlance, your re-evaluation is called *velocity*, which is roughly the number of features that can be delivered over a period of time. At the start, you have no idea what your team's velocity is, thus your agreement with the stakeholders. Over time, you will learn more and more about how your team delivers, and your delivery schedule will become more accurate.

The prioritized feature list ensures that your team is working on the most important features first so that when any hard deadline approaches, regardless of what's been done, you can be sure it's what's most important.

If the stakeholders want more delivered sooner, remind them of the adage that "Nine women cannot make a baby in one month." Adding more people, especially at the start, is a recipe for disaster. As part of your regular schedule re-evaluation, you should also include an evaluation of the team size. It's entirely possible that, once the project gets going, there will be tasks that can be split up amongst more developers. Being open to this is part of the deal, but you should insist that the project start small.

This will naturally lead to a discussion of how the project will be delivered. It's important that everyone understand the process by which features will be developed and made available.

Delivery Process

At a high level, stakeholders need a way to know what's going on with the project. They will naturally be curious about what's been built, how it's going, and if the team is still on schedule. While you don't want to be constantly burdened with "status reports", it's in your best interest to be open and honest about the project (especially if things haven't been going well).

Many agile methodologies suggest weekly demonstrations of the work that has been done. Other methodologies suggest demoing features whenever they are "ready". What both of these techniques have in common is that stakeholders are frequently shown working parts of the system. Rather than reacting to a stakeholder's need for status, you must be proactive in showing them what you and your team have accomplished.

If the stakeholders aren't going to be deeply involved with the project day-to-day, I'd still recommend a regular demonstration of what the team has accomplished. It should be weekly or more frequent. This could be a brief meeting to show the feature, an email of what features have been completed, or a screencast showing how things work. Set up whatever is going to be most useful to everyone, but that will not put undue burden on you and your team to prepare.

If an iterative approach is not part of your company's culture, you can still work this way, and I'd recommend it. If the stakeholders prefer fewer checkpoints on the status of the project, they can certainly have them, while you continue to iterate quickly. Your demo days can simply be to the team and anyone interested and serve as an internal rallying point for maintaining momentum.

Once you've established the "external rhythm" of your team, you should agree on how internal progress will be tracked, or how to otherwise keep features organized. Some teams use index cards taped to a wall, others use complex tracking software such as JIRA. As with demo days, your goal is get high value for low effort. If you use an issue-tracking system, keep the fields to a minimum and do not create complex workflows. All you need is a way to see your features in priority order, to indicate who's working on them, and to know if a feature is in-progress, complete, or not-yet-started.

You should also agree on a very high-level source control policy. Basically, you want everyone to agree on what and when to commit to source control. You should have a good idea of when to use branches and when to merge them to the master branch (another option is *feature toggles*, which allow codepaths to be dynamically turned on or off, allowing multiple features to be in development in the same branch of code. Developers simply toggle their feature on when it's ready). Don't set up anything too complicated. Your primary goal is to allow deploying the application with whatever features are complete, even if several features are currently in-development.

If your source control system supports branching and merging, the simplest thing is to put each feature on its own branch, and merge them to the main branch when they are complete. If your source control system doesn't support these features, it'll be a bit more complicated. You'll need to make sure that the master branch is always deployable and runnable.

Once you've covered these basics, you'll move on to bootstrapping the application itself, which was covered in chapter 8.

After this is done, you and your team are ready to start delivery. You have a good understanding of what problem you'll be solving, a basic schedule for when you'll deliver, a process that everyone understands for deliver, and a minimum deployable application ready to receive features.

12.2   Deliver the Project

As team lead, you have to do more than just deliver code. You'll need to shepherd the team through the development process, ensure that the conventions and policies the team has established are being followed (and are still suitable), review code, and communicate with project stakeholders.

You can accomplish much of this via a short, weekly meeting with the team and stakeholders. Beyond that, you should review as much code as you can that's going into the application.

Weekly Team Meeting

You've hopefully chosen a lightweight, iterative delivery process. Your job is to make sure that the process is being followed and that it is still appropriate. Regardless of the specifics of the process, the goal is to make sure the team is working, that they are working on the right features, and that project stakeholders understand how much progress has been made.

The simplest way to do this is to have a regular weekly team meeting. It should be no more than 60 minutes and can serve many of your goals as lead without requiring too much preparation or distraction by the team.

A weekly meeting also serves to establish the rhythm of the project, which is crucial for maintaining momentum and giving everyone the feeling that progress is being made.

You should run the meeting yourself - ideally on a Monday morning - with the following agenda:

1. Review/demonstrate features delivered since the last meeting. In the early stages of the project, you should do all the demoing yourself, even for features you didn't build. Keep the demos extremely short and very tight. This will require preparation on your end, but will keep you from wasting everyone's time in the meeting. Later in the project, have developers demo their own features, now that you've established a baseline for demos.

2. Each developer spends 30 seconds explaining what they are working on and explicitly acknowledging that if are (or are not) blocked on completion. You need to know if there is something standing between any developer and their ability to deliver results. Meet individually with anyone who's blocked after the meeting; do not discuss specific during the meeting as they are not relevant to the entire group of attendees (in more formal agile processes, this is how a daily standup meeting is conducted).

3. Update the delivery schedule. If you have hard deadlines, update your estimate as to which features will be available by those deadlines.

4. List the next several features in the priority list that will be worked on. Confirm with the stakeholders that these are still in the correct priority.

5. Finish with any general announcements or other team-wide information.

This meeting is spending many peoples' valuable time not doing their primary job, so you want to keep it short and to the point. The purpose is to exchange factual information and identify potential roadblocks. Any specific issues or points of detailed discussion should be taken "offline" and discussed after the meeting by only those parties who are interested.

In particular, if certain features won't be available by the hard deadlines in the schedule, you need to have that discussion outside this meeting. Your available options are to rearrange which features get built in which order. If additional team members can help, say so, but if they cannot, make that clear.

Treat requests to "work harder" as non-sequiters: the team is working as hard as they can. Do not promise to "try" to meet the deadline anyway. You are the expert here and are giving the stakeholders an honest assessment of the project's status, as promised initially. Remind them that they agreed to consider the original estimate inaccurate in exchange for regular, honest feedback.

This can be the most difficult task you're likely to face, so being highly organized and confident is the way through. Be prepared before any weekly meeting where you will be telling the stakeholders that the schedule needs to be adjusted. Stand firm and be as logical and dispassionate as you can. The company is paying for your expertise and your team is relying on you to accurately represent their capabilities.

As ever, be solutions and results-oriented. Avoid discussions around "why" the project is "late". The project actually isn't "late", because that would assume a detailed schedule and firm commitment exists, where none does. Whatever you do, do not leave the conversation with stakeholders expecting something you know cannot be delivered. The book "The Clean Coder" has some great information on handling situations like this (see the reading list in appendix E).

Your weekly meeting will take care of many of your ongoing duties, but you also have to understand what's going into the codebase. The only way to do that is via regular code reviews.

Code Reviews

Code reviews are one of the few techniques proven to detect bugs and improve code quality. They are also very easy to integrate into your process and you can get a lot of out of them via a simple asynchronous process. In other words, you can reap the benefits of code review without having a lot of extra meetings.

Code reviews also create a sense of *collective code ownership*, which is a concept from Extreme Programming (XP). The idea is that when the team feels like the code belongs to "everyone", no one person is discouraged from contributing or understanding any part of the code. This leads to widespread knowledge of the codebase, which allows anyone to work on anything.

Early in the project, you should review all code, or at least be a participant in all code reviews. As the project moves forward, you can dial back your involvement to only crucial features or for new team members' work, and allow the stronger members of your team to handle the bulk of the code reviews.

The basic process for doing a code review is as follows:

1. When a developer has completed a feature, the code implementing it is submitted for review. The form this takes depends on the tools you are using. It could be a diff against the master branch or a pull request to merge a feature branch.

2. The reviewers are notified and examine the code. If you have a dedicated tool, the reviewers should be able to comment on particular bits of the code and start discussion around particular issues. If you do

not have a tool, reviewers should use email and reference file names and line numbers. You want this to be asynchronous so that many can be involved without scheduling a meeting.

3. The code author should respond to issues and discussion and make changes that are needed based on the feedback. These changes should be a new set of diffs against the code under review, so that reviewers can easily see what the updates are.

4. Once the author and reviewers are happy with the state of the code, it can be merged into the main trunk.

As a reviewer, your goals out of any given code review are:

- Identify bugs

- Identify obvious security and performance issues

- Code cleanliness

- Verify adherence to, or establishment of, consistent style guidelines

The first two issues' importance are obvious, but the second two issues bear a bit more discussion as they are important to the long-term health of the project.

Code Cleanliness

Slop that goes to production will likely never be cleaned up, and will certainly not be cleaned up by the developer that made the mess. During the review - before the code ships - is the absolute best time to address these issues. This is because everything is in everyone's head in terms of how the code works, what the variables, classes, functions, and methods all do, as well as what the code is for.

Hopefully, your team is on board with keeping code clean, and are fine with making changes to make code easier to maintain. Clean code is of most benefit to you as the team lead, because you are ultimately responsible for the code. As long as you are team lead, you must be ready to work on any part of the project's codebase at a moment's notice.

Checking for code cleanliness is one of the reasons I'm recommending you review all code during the initial phases of the project. This is a chance for you to establish your expectations around the quality of the code. Don't be too onerous, however. The team needs to be delivering value, so there are diminishing returns on "polishing" code.

Adherence to Style

When you started the project, you likely established some conventions as to where files go, how to name classes, etc. As you work, you will want to enhance this style guide so that more of the "decisions that don't matter but must be made" are made.

When you identify new patterns for which a convention might need to be created, comment on these, asking the code's author opinion. For example, in section 8.5, we discussed avoiding creating a naming convention for database triggers until you actually needed a trigger. If you turn out to need database triggers, ask the author of the trigger if the naming scheme that was chosen should the team's new convention for trigger names.

It's not important that you make these decisions. Having them made by someone other than you can give the team a feeling of ownership over the code and its conventions. The team will eventually feel collective ownership over the code's style and it won't seem like orders enforced from on-high.

General Tips on Reviewing Code

Having your code reviewed can be difficult. You've spent a lot of time making the code do what you need it to and perhaps a fair amount of care in crafting it. Having someone else "tear it to shreds" can be hard to stomach, especially if you are an inexperienced developer or a developer who has never had their code reviewed.

As the tech lead, you don't want your team to feel dread at having their code reviewed, or to fear what might happen when they submit their code for review. Code reviews aren't just meant to increase the quality of the code, they are also a great learning experience for everyone.

This is the other reason you should be involved in each review early on. You want to set a positive and encouraging tone, and you want to make sure everyone else does, too.

Here are some guidelines that I have found useful in performing and participating in code reviews:

Read the entire changeset before commenting on it As you read the code, issues may jump out. Do not comment on them initially. Often, some issues are not as serious (or are not issues at all) when you understand the entire change.

Further, if the developer's overall approach is flawed, for example the design will not work or needs major refactoring, you don't want to waste time on line-level comments. In this case, you want to make a general comment on the diff as to the problem, and request a refactoring or rework.

It's crucial that you are constructive and instructive. Indicate specifically what the issue is, how you might address it, and why your suggestion is an improvement.

189

Do *not* do this as a "command", but rather a suggestion. For example, "What I would do here is to use composition along with a set of strategies rather than inheritance". You want the code author on your side with what the issues are, but you want them to have the chance to fix it on his own.

Speak about the code, not the coder Depersonalizing the code makes issues feel less like an attack and more of a technical discussion. Consider this Java code:

```java
public Collection<Address> getAddresses(
    Collection<Customer> customers) {

  List<Address> addresses =
    new ArrayList<Address>();

  for(Customer customer: customers) {
    if (!addresses.contains(
        customer.getAddress())
      ) {
      addresses.add(customer.getAddress());
    }
  }
}
```

The problem with this code is that the developer should've used a Set, which automatically strips duplicates. Your instinctual comment might be "why did you use a List instead of a Set?" This makes the comment about the coder, implying that *the coder* is wrong. Instead, talk about the code more directly, for example: "If we used a Set instead of a List, we could skip the duplicate check."

This does two things: first, it speaks about the code as if it were written by the team, enforcing collective code ownership. Second, it suggests a course of action and the reason for the suggestion. The initial comment ("why not use a Set?") carries this information only implicitly. If the reason for using a Set were so obvious to the code's author, they would've used it in the first place.

If you don't understand something, ask Your code reviews focus heavily on producing an understandable code base. You are optimizing for read-time, not write-time convenience. If code is confusing, it needs to change, but you don't want to jump straight to "this is confusing, make it more clear".

Instead, start from the assumption that the code author knows best, and has done their best to make the code clean and clear. Instead, ask a pointed question for clarification.

Approach style-related issues tactfully When commenting on stylistic issues or issues related to code cleanliness, you have to be careful. These are much more subjective issues, and you can end up "bikeshedding" issues, arguing for personal preference instead of adherence to an agreed-upon style guide. You want to focus on *just* the style guide and, when discussing issues of code cleanliness, be as objective as you can.

If the code author writes some code that adheres to the guide, but just "isn't how you'd do it", resist the urge to comment. For minor-but-important issues, indicate in your comments that you understand the issue is minor, but is still interesting discussing briefly.

For example, consider this Ruby code:

```ruby
ip6_only = ip_addresses.select { |block|
  block.ip6?
}
```

The name `block` is poorly chosen, because most ruby code uses the variable name `block` for a code block passed into a method. In dynamic languages like Ruby, naming conventions are important because there is no way to know the type of something simply by reading the code.

In the grand scheme of things, this isn't actually that big of a deal, but if the author doesn't feel strongly about the name, it's worth changing now. I'd use a comment like this: "I know it's a nitpick, but can you choose a different name than `block`, since most Rubyists will think it's a block and not IP address. What about `ip_address`?"

Since the review is being conducted electronically, tone cannot be conveyed, so contextualizing your comments can make it easier for developers to understand your intent.

Finally, if there is a disagreement about style, you should err on the side of the developer who will be maintaining the code (as discussed in section 4.6).

Don't be afraid to have a real-time conversation When conducting "asynchronous" code reviews, it can be difficult for everyone to be objective, especially when the team members don't know each other very well. If you find difficulty or pushback in the process, consider doing some reviews "real-time" either sitting at the same desk, or over video conference (or even instant messenger). With an established team, it can also be a good idea to do in-person reviews for newly-added team members, as it eases them into the process.

Convey this information to others Eventually (and likely initially), other developers will also be involved with code reviews. If you see them writing code review comments that are too personal or adversarial, it needs to stop immediately. Start from the assumption that the developer in question is trying to do the right thing. Let them know that we need to make things about the code and not the coder. Give them some suggestions about how the comments could be re-stated to be less adversarial.

In addition to reviewing the work your team is producing, and informing project stakeholders of how things are going, you will often be required to interact with other technical departments, such as Quality Assurance (QA) and Security.

Interacting with QA

If your company has a Quality Assurance (QA) team, or you have someone from that team assigned to your project, you will need to incorporate them into your process.

Since you and your team are using unit and acceptance tests to drive your work, QA should not (generally speaking) be finding bugs. If QA has a strict, pre-defined role in your company, simply let them do their work against a QA server to which you are deploying, or on one managed by the QA team.

If QA's role is less clearly defined, the best thing they can do for you is to do system-level user-based testing. They should use the entire system as a user would, trying to do things that users do that software engineers don't anticipate. This is extremely useful if your project will interface with existing applications; the QA team can set up all the applications and connect your app and see how it behaves in more conventional use.

This sort of testing can be very difficult to use for driving work, as the tests are hard to automate, brittle, and slow. QA also don't have their heads deep in the project space and will not have the same set of assumptions about how the system should work. This means they'll find bugs you and your team didn't anticipate.

If your project hasn't been launched, I'd recommend deploying features as they are done (or at the end of each week) and not waiting for QA to "bless" features. If QA finds bugs, roll them into your priorities. The problem with having QA act as a gatekeeper is that every bug requires a discussion to determine if it should "hold up" the release.

Unless your team is producing extremely low-quality work, it's far more efficient to release the code as-is, and have a separate discussion about bug priorities in the context of the feature list. It's highly likely that the project stakeholders will prefer the team to work on the next important feature, rather than fix minor bugs. If you bring the conversation back to the business value of the features - the results you're paid to deliver - this will focus everyone on the right thing.

As we'll see later, you'll revisit this decision once the project has launched, since bugs can have a higher cost when users are actively using the system.

Interacting with a Security Team

Basic security should be considered in everything you do. I would recommend configuring some sort of automated security scanning as part of your continuous integration process and to not consider any feature complete if it causes security warnings.

Beyond that, there may be additional security concerns which were hopefully identified up front. Based on those issues, you should have a good idea how involved the security team - if any - will be with your project.

Depending on your organization and your project, they may be approvers and gatekeepers, the same as QA, or they may just need to be "in the loop". Include them as necessary based on that. Always be cognizant of the value of their suggestions. Security issues are like bugs: some are more crucial to fix than any particular feature, while others are not worth the time. Focus on the results you need to deliver and the consequences of security holes being exploited.

Once the initial set of features has been delivered (which may coincide with an official launch), the project is "done" and will go into maintenance mode[1]. Maintenance mode could be continuing to deliver high-value features or it could be to simply fix bugs that crop up.

12.3 Enhance the Project and Fix Bugs

After the initial delivery of an application, work on it will continue, based on many factors. Sometimes, the application is considered "feature complete" and a small team is assigned to fix bugs and perform security updates. Other times, a dedicated team will be assigned to the application to continually add new features and enhance the software.

As team lead, this mostly boils down to how many people are going to be assigned to work on the application and how much of their time will be available. For a feature complete application, it might be one part time person. For an application that will be continually enhanced, it could be your entire project team.

The way you delivered features during the initial build of the app will work perfectly well for maintaining the project. The only real difference is that users are using the application, so you need to take them into account in terms of deploying new features. QA's role might also be different.

After the application launches, get together with the project stakeholders and the QA lead assigned to your team. Your

---

[1]I'm not saying the application itself is done. Software, generally speaking, is never done; it just has, or doesn't have, particular features. The *project*, was to deliver certain features. Therefore, it can be "done"

goal is agree on how new features and bugfixes will be deployed to users. Ideally, features and bugfixes can be pushed to production whenever they are ready (the "continuous deployment" scenario). If that is unacceptable, push for no less than a weekly release and agree on an "emergency push" procedure to allow for immediate release of important bugfixes.

You will also need to decide if QA will act as a gatekeeper for new features and fixes. The right answer here depends on the project and the risk of pushing bugs into production. If you are operating under continuous deployment for an application that is not life threatening or highly critical, there's little value in holding features for QA approval. If, on the other hand, a mistake could end up costing the company significant time or money, the extra eyes on any changes could reduce this risk.

Once a project has been launched, you may operate as team lead for the application for quite some time. Eventually, either to work on a new project or for a new company, you'll leave the project.

12.4   Leave the Project

Your last duty as team lead is to leave an ongoing project in capable hands. This is a good thing for you personally, as it leaves everyone with a positive impression of your time as lead. It also ensures that the company continues to get value out of the team during the changeover.

Although there is likely documentation the new lead can pore over to get up to speed, there is likely information *not* in any document that only you as the lead understand. Your job is to pass that information onto the new lead and publicly acknowledge the change in leadership.

Schedule a one-on-one with the new lead to go over what they'll need to know. Ask them to review all available documentation beforehand, such as the coding style guide, delivery process, and other system documentation. Answer any questions they have about this information.

Next, you want the new lead to be aware of any current or potential issues with the team or application. For example, if a particular area of the application is a source for bugs, let them know. If certain developers on the team require more scrutiny during reviews, make sure they know that as well. Be sure to also indicate which developers are particularly reliable or effective; the new team lead will need to rely on the top performers to get up to speed.

After your one-on-one, you need to "pass the torch" to the new lead. The simplest way to do this is at the start of your next weekly team meeting. Start the meeting by announcing the new team lead, making sure the team knows you have confidence in their new lead and wish them luck.

12.5   Moving On

This brings us to the end of our journey through the career of a software developer. We've learned some great techniques for fixing bugs, implementing complex features, creating entirely new applications, and leading a team of developers. By following the processes we've outlined, you will distinguish yourself as a valuable member of your team and company.

Many fields have a professional "code of conduct" and, some day, software development may have one, too. It's my hope that, if it must, it's similar to what I've outlined, as these techniques have worked for me throughout my career, and worked well for many others.

Until that day, the best we can do to make our profession better is to lead by example. By following processes that lead to clean, maintainable code and applications, we communicate to others that quality software can be written quickly. It's my firm belief that this will make our profession - and the world that depends so much on software - a much better place.

13

Conclusion

We now come to the end of our journey. You've learned how to be better in every way at being a developer. From a simple process for quickly fixing bugs, to a larger process for building features, all the way to building apps from scratch and leading teams, you should be relatively able to handle any of development task.

We've also touched on more "soft" aspects of being a developer: making a technical argument, working with others, and communicating with non-technical people. These skills are just as important (if not more-so) than actually coding up features. You don't work alone, and your ability to work with others is the key to your success.

Each step of the way, we avoided getting too specific. The ideas here are more of a framework than a step-by-step guide. Your next steps are to fill in these steps with your own style and your own way of doing things. Much like the conventions we establish when creating a new application, **how** you approach being a senior software engineer isn't nearly as important as that you **do** approach it.

To agree with this book is to agree to care about your career, its place in your company, and its place in our community. You're deciding to be better. You're deciding to be amazing.

A

Engineer as Product Manager

If I could sum up the best programmers I've worked with in a sentence, it would be:

> They know what to build and they know how build it

The later is almost trivial to achieve compared to the former, but without both, you won't be doing your best work.

I've only recently come to understand how equally important both building "software right" and building the "right software" are. As a young engineer, working as a consultant or at the bottom of an org-chart, I was given things to build so I built them. "Knowing how to build" was all it seemed I needed to know.

Fortunately, getting good at knowing how to build software is straightforward (if time consuming). It just takes experience and practice, and there are myriad tools, techniques, and other resources to help (this book is one of those resources).

Knowing *what* to build, however, is more difficult.

A.1 Knowing What to Build

Knowing what software to build requires specialized knowledge beyond software development. In general sense, you have to understand what problem exists that needs solving. You then have to evaluate all the ways in which that problem could be solved (with or without software). Then, you have to weigh those solutions against a variety of constraints: time, money, chance of success, cost of failure, etc.

Unlike building software, the processing of deciding *what* to build is not that generalizable. You must have specific knowledge of the domain in question as well as access to data about the organization you're working for. My (limited) understanding of the utility industry while working at Opower in no way prepared me for working at Stitch Fix, where I was required to understand retail, logistics, and women's fashion.

On most teams, the developers aren't expected to understand the domain at a deep level, and product managers are employed to translate business problems into software requirements.

A.2 Enter the Product Manager

The way most teams deal with balancing what to build against how to build it is to separate the work to specialists. On one side, you have developers who are great at building software. On the other are product managers (sometimes called "business analysts") that understand the domain as well as the specific business. The two teams are intended to work together: product managers identify the right problems to solve and developers write software to solve them.

This is a nice idea, but has practical problems. The product manager is rarely technical enough to understand software at a detailed level. Even when they are (for example, a former developer who moved into product management), they have no real skin in the game to actually develop the solution. Whatever decisions they make, it's the *developers* who will deal with the consequences of those decisions.

The developers, lacking a deep understanding of the domain and business, will tend to propose solutions that favor their team over solving the underlying problem (which is likely not completely clear to them). They tend to propose solutions that:

- are easy to build and maintain, even if they don't fully solve the problem.

- are more interesting to work on than a more optimal solution.

- use new technology, putting the solution at risk, also known as "Résumé-Driven-Development"

I've done all of these things myself, and seen talented programmers to the same. And without a complete understanding of the problem domain, who can blame them?

When developers complain about being treated as replaceable parts, this is precisely why that treatment happens. Developers proposing solutions without a solid understanding of the problem being solved are not acting like partners; they are acting like ticket-takers. It's demoralizing to be a ticket-taker and you aren't going to do your best work this way.

In several chapters of this book, we talked about processes for writing software–from bug fixing to feature deliver to greenfield applications. Each time, we started with "understand the problem". In the context of getting particular features built or bugs fixed, this step is crucial in making sure you do the right thing.

What we're talking about here is larger. When you start to think more about the problems you are solving and less about how you're going to solve them, you move from being a code monkey to becoming a partner.

A.3   Be a Partner

One the one hand, there are product managers who necessarily lack the technical skills (and accountability) to understand technical decisions. On the other hand, there are engineers who don't have a complete understanding of the domain and the problems being solved. The result is the wrong software being delivered and problems going either unsolved or being solved incorrectly.

Someone has to meet in the middle.

Although acquiring technical proficiency is straightforward, it's incredibly time-consuming. It's not uncommon to encounter developers with years of experience who feel they've only scratched the surface of how to effectively write software. As such, there's no reasonable way a product manager can gain sufficient knowledge and experience in programming to help.

But, understanding the problem domain, the important problems to solve, and *why* they are important is much simpler. While a developer might never be as great a product manager as a dedicated person, learning the domain and taking a product perspective can be a force-multiplier for the team. A "developer-as-product-manager", even when working with a dedicated product manager, will be "building the right things".

If you can become that developer, you'll be doing your best work.

A.4 Doing Your Best Work

Let's come back to those developers I mentioned at the start of this essay. Although technically skilled, they weren't necessarily programming wizards. What made them effective was that they took the time to understand the problem being solved. They took the time to understand what measurable impact a solution might have, and why it was important. They learned about the specifics of the business where they worked.

And they were doing their best work. They were engaged with what they were doing. They delivered results and could point to the positive impact their work had on the organization.

When developers understand why they are doing what they're doing **and** have a way to know that what they did achieved its goals, everyone benefits. The organization gets more optimal solutions and the development team is much happier. Instead of acting like (and being treated like) ticket-takers, the developers are treated as partners.

And partners are trusted.

Instead of pressured to deliver something quickly, a *trusted* team can have honest conversations about delivery schedules. A *trusted* team doesn't have to justify their every technical decision to someone who can't understand it. A *trusted* team doesn't spend a lot of time getting "permission" to work a particular way. A *trusted* team spends most of its time building great software that solves real problems and has a measurable impact.

Who wouldn't want to work on that team?

The only thing such a team needs to do is to spend time understanding their place in the organization–what problems the team exists to solve. Figuring this out can be tricky.

A.5   Find Out Your Team's Purpose

To get an understanding of the problems your team exists to solve, you need to connect what your team does directly to the goals of the organization. Ideally, you can point to the features you build, and show how they affect the data used by the company's decision-makers.

For example, I once worked on software to support warehouse logistics. The software was designed to assist workers in a warehouse in finding items to ship to customers. The goal was to make the workers more efficient so that, as the business scaled, proportionally fewer workers would be needed.

We built the software and it worked as desired. I was able to connect something I worked on directly to numbers on a spreadsheet that the management team of the company used in assessing the business.

It may not be this simple at your current job. It might even be impossible. Start asking questions. Find out about what you're doing and why. Talk to the people involved about how they work and how they make decisions.

Be warned, however. If your company culture is such that you get pushback or roadblocks to merely *understanding* how the company works, start polishing your résumé. You are not positioned to do your best work in such a place.

In this extreme case, you'll be faced with a tougher decision about where you *can* go to do your best work. Fortunately, as a skilled programmer, you are privileged to exist in a world that holds your skills in very high demand. With some basic legwork, there's a good chance you can find a great place to work where you can be a partner, instead of a ticket-taker.

My recommendation is to find a product company that sells its product directly to the product's users. The business model of such a company is very easy to understand. Everything a direct-to-consumer product company does can be traced to reducing cost or increasing/protecting revenue. All you need to learn is the specifics of the company's line of business.

I'm not saying that you can't do your best work at an enterprise software company, a non-profit, or as a consultant. I'm just saying that if you want to start getting good at knowing *what* software to build, you want to start off simple, and a business model based on direct sales tends to be pretty simple.

Whatever you do, start asking yourself (and others) *why* you are building what you are building. What problem does it solve? What other solutions were evaluated?

Become curious about more than just technology and you'll start doing your best work.

B

Production is All That Matters

Software is only as useful as the effects it has. Beautiful code, sitting in a version control repository, never deployed, and never used is far worse than the results of a 24-hour hack-fest that's actually running somewhere.

Your software running in a production environment is the literal results we've talked the entire book about how to deliver. How your software runs in production is almost **all that matters**.

Further, your skills as a developer will be severely lacking if you don't understand how your code actually runs, serving actual users, doing its actual job. If you never find out what your code is doing on production, and if you aren't *responsible* for how it works on production, you're never going to be much more than a typist.

If you find yourself in this situation, don't worry, it's not necessarily your fault. Many organizations don't allow developers any real access to production. Many organizations have operations staff who support applications in production. Much like the divide between product manager and programmer, there is inherent inefficiency in having one person write software for another to support in production.

B.1 "DevOps"

The concept of "devops" is a way to try to bridge the divide between operations and engineering. Even the highest-functioning team is still going to have problems. How can an operations person whose expertise is in servers, understand why a missing edge case in user sign-up is causing exceptions? How can someone specializing in tuning virtual machines diagnose issues related to errors from your payment processor? How can an expert in Linux administration understand that there's bad data in the database?

Realistically, they can't. The operations staff can't have a deep understanding of the business requirements of your application to the point where they can diagnose problems. The fact is, the person who wrote the code is in the best position to understand why it might not be working and why it's causing problems. The operations team provides a reliable environment in which the app can run, but it's the programmers that must support the applications *behavior*.

To get there requires a simple four-step process, based around *production errors*. A production error is anything unexpected that happens in your application. This is roughly equivalent to an unhandled exception, but it could be more than that, such as bad data in the database, or a codepath that "should never" happen.

The four steps are:

1. Understand why handling production errors is important

2. Detect production errors

3. Fix production errors

4. Avoid production errors

Let's go over each one in detail.

B.2 Handling Production Errors Matters

Your application serves a purpose. It meets the needs of its users. When it encounters a problem, it fails to meet that need. When your application fails to meet the need of a user, revenue could be lost. In other words, when your application experiences a failure, you are putting the business at risk.

Let's take an example. Suppose that every time a user signs up, they must activate their account by clicking on a link sent by an automated email from your application. Suppose a user signs up and, at the exact moment the welcome email is to be sent, there is a network error and the email isn't sent.

The user will never get their activation email unless steps are taken. If no steps are taken, this customer won't use your service, which means you aren't making money from them. This user *could* have been a happy customer, even one that was an advocate for your company, driving many more customers to you but, because of an un-handled error on production, we'll never know.

This customer could call up customer service and ask why they didn't get their sign-up email. Customer service could manually activate them but this has a cost, too. Handling this means not handling something else. If it piles up, you'll need more customer service people and that, too, costs money.

All because a very basic production error wasn't handled.

211

You may think that a few missing users won't matter in the grand scheme of things. Aside from being bad customer service and a poor corporate policy, it's also foolish and lazy thinking. Every customer matters. Someone wants to pay the company money, your job as a developer is to make sure there's no software standing in their way. And don't think the rules are different for users of "internal apps". If their jobs are inefficient because of buggy software, they will cost more, and the business will be less successful.

Dismissing errors like this sets a dangerous precedent. You must begin to make judgement calls. Which production errors *matter*? How many failures is "too many"? How much loss of revenue/increase in cost is it OK for the engineering team to create before something needs to be done?

All failures matter, *one* is too many, and the engineering team should not tolerate loss of revenue or increased costs due to software issues. Engineers are paid a lot of money to solve problems and should treat losses in revenue caused by their solutions seriously.

You want a culture of fault-tolerance and responsiveness. To get that, you'll need to set up systems to detect production errors, create procedures for handling them, and adjust the way you work to account for them and prevent them from happening.

A culture of fault-tolerance means thinking a bit harder about what you're doing than maybe you would otherwise. It means being a bit more paranoid about what might happen in production. Mostly, however, it means gaining an understanding of how your application behaves in production, and making it a priority to improve its behavior.

The first step to fault-tolerant software is to detect errors in production.

B.3 Detecting Production Errors

A software application is nothing more than a complex input/output device. Information comes in, processing happens, and output is returned. Inexperienced developers primarily focus on input from and output to the software's users. You need to do more. You need, at the very least, some output that is just for you, the developer, to understand how the software is running.

The most basic developer-targeted output is the application log.

Your Application Log

Making use of this log requires two things:

- Sensible & judicious logging of useful information throughout your application

- A searchable, durable location for those logs

Useful Logging Messages

Your log statements should have, at a minimum:

- **Timestamp** - precisely when did this information get logged? Preferably, to the nanosecond or millisecond

- **Severity** - a way to record the seriousness of the events that led to the log message. Typical values are error, warning, info, and debug

- **Process identifier** - a way to unambiguous identify the server and process that generated the log message

- **Request identifier** - a way to identify all messages generated as part of a single request. For a web-based application, this value would be assigned by the web

213

server and made available in the application's environment. Your logging software can pull this value out and include it in the log message. This allows you to trace a particular call from start to finish.

- **Some use information** - a description of what you'd like to know if things go wrong or if some code path executes. Likely, you'll want database identifiers and descriptions of what is happening or why.

Log every request and what the response was, along with anything else that's relevant to what went on during the request. Log edge cases in your logic, warnings, or other events that are outside the "happy path". You might also log the results of complex calculations whose results are important.

Don't worry about performance - you can remove logging if you need to, but your primary duty is to understand how your application is working, and the log is a great place to do that.

These logs must be aggregated somewhere so you can search them.

A Searchable Location for Logs

Without the ability to search logs, they are useless. If they are sitting on a disk you have access to, open up the man page for grep and have at it. More likely, you'll need them in some sort of log aggregator like Splunk, Loggly, or PaperTrail. These allow sophisticated searches in a web interface.

This is where your operations staff can be helpful. Although they aren't in a position to necessarily understand the *contents* of your logs, they will be able to set up a general management solution for them, accouting for the ever-growing size of the files.

The main advantage of these systems over grep is that you can easily share log results with others, including nontechnical but technically-minded folks who may be involved in diagnosing a production error.

Your log aggregator can also be hooked into your second developer output stream, which is alerting.

Alerting

An alert is a push notification that an event requiring action has occurred.

That sentence is a lot more dense that it appears and each part of it is crucial for effective alerting. Let's break it down:

- *push notification* - you get an email, a popup, an SMS, a page, a siren, whatever. Something you can't ignore that is sent to you. This isn't something you must remember to check. The form of the notification might be related to its severity (e.g. the site being down might page you, but an un-handled exception will email you).

- *an event has occurred* - something has happened that shouldn't have. This could be a particular branch of complex logic (e.g. /* this should never happen */), or it could be the result of an external process checking for system invariants (e.g. a SQL script you run hourly to look for bad data in the database).

- *requires some action* - because of this event, you must take action or loss of revenue/increase in cost will occur. This implies that non-actionable events should not generate alerts. You want alerts to be something you pay attention to and not something you start ignoring. By all means, log non-actionable events, but do not alert if no action needs to (or can) be taken.

We'll see how to turn non-actionable events into alerts when we talk about application statistics.

For proper alerting, you need three things:

- A system to manage sending and cataloging alerts
- A way in your application code to trigger an alert
- A way to trigger alerts from outside your application code

An example of an alerting system is Airbrake. Another example is /bin/mail. You might need multiple systems. For example, you may use Pager Duty for application alerting, but use PingDom for general website availability alerting. The fewer the better, but you need all alertable events covered.

Triggering an alert depends on the system you are using, but, at the very least, you need a catch-all exception handler that triggers an alert whenever an exception occurs that your code doesn't handle.

Finally, you need an easy way to write monitoring scripts that trigger your alerting system. This is because you should start writing scripts that assert invariants about your environment and alert when those invariants are no longer true.

For example, your database might store records of customer purchases. You might further store, for successful purchases, what the credit card authorization code was. If you have a successful purchase, but no credit card authorization code, something is wrong. That should never happen.

Of course it *will* happen, so you should write a script that checks all successful purchases for an authorization code (e.g. any purchase that has been in a successful state for more than a few minutes, but that doesn't have an authorization code), and trigger an alert for any that don't have one. Someone might be getting something for free. Loss of revenue.

One final note: do not ignore alerts. If you are filtering out or ignoring alerts, you are not doing your job. You are ignoring your system telling you that it's not doing what you've designed it to do. If you have so many alerts that you are overwhelmed with them, you either have a terrible system, or you are alerting for non-actionable events. Fix those issues before reaching for your email filters. Fix them before adding features, because your business is starting to tank.

In addition to the output you show the user, and the logging output you create for yourself, there is a third output stream. This output stream is an analytic on the events occurring in your system and is a way to turn non-actionable events into actionable ones. For example, a 404 is not an actionable event. However, 5,000 over the course of 2 minutes might be. You need statistics.

Application Statistics

Application statistics represent a set of vital signs for your application. They indicate, at a high level, what's going on inside your system. A statistic might be the number of 404 responses per unit time. Another might be the number of broken builds. You could get statistics on the number of purchases made, or the number of user logins. Anything and everything.

To set up this output stream, you need three things:

- A system to manage your statistics

217

- A way to send statistics to this system from your application without negatively impacting performance *or* causing production errors

- A way to send statistics from outside your application code

A common tool for managing statistics is Graphite. A common tool for sending them is Statsd. You could also use specially-formatted log messages and grep.

With these tools, you "stat" information inside your application, and write external scripts that run periodically to stat other things as well. The more the merrier, because you don't know what you're going to need.

Note that this isn't like tracking website activity, signup conversions, or A/B test results. Those things are important, but they are not what we're talking about.

Once you have some statistics set up, you can then observe your application's "rhythm" over time. Hopefully, you'll see a "normal" usage pattern. For example, the system I work on now will show a spike around noon Pacific time when the US Postal Service drops off returned merchandise to our warehouse.

Once you have *this*, you can then **alert** if certain statistics are out of whack. This is definitely "Advanced Band", and not something worth setting up for brand new projects, but it can be really useful. For example, if you see a drastic drop in purchases or a spike in customer service tickets, you'll know something's wrong.

Now that we can use logs, alerting, and statistics to find out about production errors, we need to know how to fix them when they happen. And fix them, we must.

B.4 Fixing Production Errors

Production errors must be addressed immediately. There are two reasons for this:

- It eliminates any judgment from your remediation procedure - production errors can lead to a loss of revenue or increased costs, so addressing them should be your highest priority. Time spent thinking about the seriousness of the problem or the time tradeoffs is money slipping away. Don't think, react.

- By allowing production errors to interrupt your workflow, you become motivated to write more fault-tolerant code, because that is the only way to actually reduce production errors. We'll get to that in the next section.

How do we address production errors? It depends on the nature of the error, but I have a few rules of thumb:

- If the error is continuously happening, drop what you are doing and fix it. A common example is rolling out a new version of the app to production, and the application stops responding. Rollback and stop the bleeding.

- If the error is a "one-off" and has a clear remediation procedure (e.g. re-trying a background job that failed due to intermittent issues), perform the procedure immediately.

- If the error is transient but has no obvious remediation procedure, you'll have to investigate:

    - Is the state of the system now invalid, e.g. bad data in the database? If so, you'll need to manually correct it.

- What was the user's experience? Is there some intent that we can capture and manually address? (for example, a customer makes a purchase, but the system fails: we could re-make that purchase on their behalf to ensure capturing the revenue)

- Can the code that broke be enhanced to avoid this problem? If so, do it (or schedule it to be done soon).

Your results might be different, but understand the theme here: restore service by putting the system back into a valid state. More importantly, do not stop until the problem is fixed or you've handed it off to someone who will follow continue trying to restore service. Sometimes, it takes a while to recover from a production error. When you need a break, hand it off, but do not stop.

I encountered a problem once at a previous job where thousands of attempted purchases failed due to issues with our promo code back-end service. The users were all left with the impression they'd made a successful purchase discounted by the promo code they provided. Because of proper logging and alerting, we saw the problem, fixed the systems so it would stop happening, and then re-created all the customer purchases behind the scenes without them ever knowing it. We protected the revenue.

Reacting to buggy software is no fun. The second reason we fix production errors immediately is to motivate us to write more fault tolerant software. We want to avoid production errors entirely.

B.5 Avoiding Production Errors

Networks are flaky. Third-party APIs have bugs. Services don't always perform at the level promised. These cause production errors, and you *can* manually fix the problems they create. Eventually, you'll come to realize that flakiness and intermittent failures are normal. It's entirely possible that your shipping vendor's API will never behave properly and will always be slow or non-responsive. When these problems cause production errors, it means your code isn't handling behavior that should be expected and viewed as normal (even if it's annoying).

Your alerting and history around production errors should be your guide to where to start enhancing the fault-tolerance of your software. Root-cause analysis will usually lead you to where you want to start.

Let's take an example. Suppose you have a background job that charges customers a monthly fee for your service:

```
class MonthlyFeeChargingJob
  def self.perform(customer_id)
    customer = Customer.find(customer_id)
    amount   = MonthlyCharge.for_customer(customer)
    result   = ThirdPartyPayments.charge(customer_id,
                                          amount)
    if result.declined?
      ChargeFailedMailer.mail(customer_id,result)
    end
  end
end
```

We handle the two expected cases: a successful charge, and a decline. Suppose that every once in a while we get a "connection refused" exception from the call to `ThirdPartyCreditCardGateway.charge`. This will generate a production error.

We fix it by re-trying the background job. Since the network is likely working by that point, the job succeeds (remember that the *job* succeeds when it completes execution, regardless of the customer's credit card's viability to make a

221

purchase). Eventually, we will tire of performing this same action manually every time there is a problem.

How can we make this code more fault-tolerant? We could try to simply automate the manual procedure of retrying the job when it fails.

First, our job will take an optional argument to indicate how many retries there have been. This allows us to break out of the retry loop in the event of a serious and lengthly network outage. Next, we catch the particular error and perform the retry (making sure to log what is going on in case we need to investigate).

```
class MonthlyFeeChargingJob
  def self.perform(customer_id,num_attempts=0)
    customer = Customer.find(customer_id)
    amount   = MonthlyCharge.for_customer(customer)
    begin
      result = ThirdPartyPayments.charge(customer_id,
                                         amount)
      if result.declined?
        ChargeFailedMailer.mail(customer_id,result)
      end
    rescue NetworkError => ex
      logger.warn("Got #{ex.message} " +
        "charging #{customer_id}, #{charge_amount}")
      if num_attempts < 5
        perform(customer_id,num_attempts + 1)
      else
        raise
      end
    end
  end
end
```

Note that we are only rescuing one type of error from the one line of code that's causing the problem. This prevents us from applying the wrong fix to other errors that might happen (for example, if we caught all exceptions, instead of just the one raised by `ChargeFailedMailer`, we could potentially charge the customer a second time by retrying the job. Not good).

The key to fault-tolerant code is to change your definition of "normal". Many developers incorrectly differentiate the so-called "happy path" from error flows. Although this distinction is useful when breaking up your work while coding, there are three possible results from your code, and they are all "normal":

- The user did what was expected

- The user did something unexpected

- An external system did something unexpected

It's that last result that you have to now consider normal. Ask yourself what might happen if you lose the network? What if the database goes down? What if the file system fills up?

Every line of code is a ticking time-bomb. Your job is to figure out how likely it is to go off and how much damage it will do if it does.

It's somewhat of an art form to determine how much "paranoia" to apply to your code. You have to weigh the likelihood of something going wrong against the consequences of it actually happening. An unlikely scenario that won't have much of an affect is something you can not worry about, but an unlikely scenario that could be disastrous is something to consider planning for.

Fault-tolerant code is ugly. It requires a lot of conditionals. It won't look like code in programming books, screencasts, or blog entries. This is the way it has to be, and I'm sorry.

If you can't outright prevent a production error, you can often find a way to turn it into a production error that's easier to resolve. For example, consider this Rails code:

```
def update_prefs(email,best_time)
  customer.email_preferences  = email
  cutomer.best_time_to_contact = best_time
  customer.save!
end
```

If save! blows up, we have a production error, and not much to go on. It will likely be the error message straight from the database, which won't be useful. If the success of this code is crucial, we can make its failure easier to deal with:

```
def update_prefs(email,best_time)
  customer.email_preferences  = email
  cutomer.best_time_to_contact = best_time
  customer.save!
rescue => ex
  raise "Saving customer #{customer.id}s " +
        "preferences to #{email}, " +
        "#{best_time} "failed: #{ex.message}"
end
```

Now, if something goes wrong, we can recreate the effects of this code manually. We know which customer was affected and what the system was trying to do when the failure occurred.

Here's a few rules of thumb that help me know when to take extra care:

- Network connections to third-parties should be assumed flaky - code with this in mind.

- Responses from third-parties should be assumed to be garbled, unparseable, or invalid at least 10% of the time. Log exactly what you get and exactly what you sent. Proving to a third party that their code is buggy or flaky should be treated like making a court-case: be prepared to prove it beyond a reasonable doubt.

- Never ignore return values or status codes - log results if you don't know how to handle them and raise explicit errors if you *really* don't know how to handle them.

- Design your internal APIs to make fault-tolerance easy to add later. For example, returning a simple boolean for "success" is almost always wrong. Using a richer data structure allows you to add diagnostic information later if you need it.

- When you log a warning or an error, it should include the context of what was being attempted, an explanation of what went wrong, and steps for remediation.

Don't overdo it

Fault-tolerant code is about *balance*. Don't go crazy with abstractions, DSLs, frameworks, or otherwise over-the-top paranoia. Think. Observe. Know your system and strike a balanced approach. A week of developer time to avoid a production error that happens every other day might not be worth it. Your time preventing this stuff is an increased cost, too.

B.6   But it's not my job!

Even if you have a terrible relationship with your operations team, and your company forbids you any access to the production environment, you should still take head of the advice above. When your production errors are helpful, thorough, and include remediation instructions, you'll be in a good position to help fix that error if it happens. And your relationship with your operations team might start to improve.

Managing a production system is a deep topic. To learn more about it by someone who's been in the trenches much longer than I have, purchase and read Release It!, by Michael Nygard. It's well-written and highly practical.

C

Responsible Refactoring

Emboldened by tests, with the words "ruthless refactoring" in my head, I used to "improve" the codebase I was maintaining at a previous job. One day, my "cleanup" caused production to break. How could this be? I was being Agile. I was Testing. I was Merciless in my Refactoring. I had found Code Smells, dammit!

I was being irresponsible.

I'm not talking about step 4 of the basic process for fixing small bugs in section 3.1, also known as "refactoring". Refactoring code that's in development and not currently running on production is something you must absolutely do. Work clean and *write* clean code. What we're talking about is changes to existing, deployed code, running in production.

C.1   Be Careful Changing Proven Code

In the previous essay, "Production is All That Matters", I outlined the importance of code in production and how to keep it running smoothly. One thing I didn't touch on was safely changing that code.

Every change to production introduces a risk of breaking something. Any system beyond a to-do list or blog engine will have complexity that can be difficult to completely cover by tests. Integration tests are brittle and cross-system tests more so. Manual QA is the most brittle of all.

Ideally, the size of your changes should be commensurate with the size of the feature you are adding. Small features should require small changes. Large changes should be an indicator of a large or complex feature.

A pure refactoring breaks this rule completely–a refactoring adds no direct business value to the application, yet introduces risk that something will break. It's a large change for no features.

"But," you say, "refactoring bad code makes it easier to change in the future. It makes us faster later and we can deliver more business value then!"

"The future", you say? I say You Ain't Gonna Need It.

C.2 You Can't Predict the Future

You Ain't Gonna Need It (otherwise known as YAGNI) is a tenet of agile software development designed to keep us focused. If we let our imaginations run wild with features we don't know we need, we end up making our code more complex than it needs to be. Refactoring code outside the basic cycle of feature development should be viewed the same way–changes you don't know you're going to need.

How then, do we prevent our code base from rotting? How can we *ever* improve it? If we focus our efforts on demonstrable business value—the future be damned—how do we avoid having a terrible codebase that's difficult to work with?

Part of the answer to this question is why it's so important to work clean, and refactor as you work. Delivering clean solutions when you are writing the code is far better than shipping a mess and hoping to clean it up later. Clean code doesn't rot.

That said, it's still hard to get everything right the first time. There's always nasty bits of code that we wish were better.

Think about some of your own code like that for a moment. It's hard to follow, has poor naming, is ugly, and unpleasant just to think about. It's *begging* to be cleaned up.

Now suppose that for the next six months, no requirement surfaces, nor bug is found, that requires modifying that code. Is its lack of cleanliness *really* a problem?

C.3 Clean Code Is Not and End

The cleanliness of a piece of code is only relevant when we need to change it. If the code is working as desired, and doesn't need to be enhanced for new features, it makes no difference how clean it is.

You may think that cleaning up such code will save time later. This is a false economy. Think about YAGNI. All we know right now is that *we don't know* what changes are in store for the code in question. We have very little information. Certainly not enough to produce an effective refactoring. For all we know, our efforts to clean up the code will make future features *harder* to implement.

If we *do* have a change in front of us, we have more information. We know *exactly* what the code needs to do. This is the key to improving our codebase. It's not in hunting for sloppy or complex code and "cleaning it up", but in looking for economies when we have a required change to make.

C.4 Clean When You Need to Change

As we talked about in chapter 4, when faced with a new change, you form a plan of attack. Part of this plan involved examining the code we need to change. Such a plan could take one of two forms:

- Plow through, making the change as expediently as possible, changing only what's needed to ship.

- Clean up or improve the code in a way that makes the change easier, then make the change.

All you have to do is decide which approach will deliver more value more quickly. It's often the first approach, but not *always*. Occasionally, it's actually faster to clean the code up first.

And **this** is how you improve your codebase. If cleaning up the code *enables you to work faster* implementing a feature you aren't dreaming up but *actually have at hand*, refactoring shipped code is the way to go.

The beauty of this approach is that you never again need a "refactoring story" in your backlog, nor do you need to get "permission" to clean up some code. You simply do it to get your job done faster and better.

C.5 Knowing When a Refactoring Will Help

Engineers are bad at estimating, so it can be difficult to know if a refactoring will speed up a new feature's build or not. Here's some guidelines that help me determine if it's better to simply make the change, or to refactor first:

- Changes to public APIs—function, method, module, or class names—are almost never worth it, particularly in a dynamically typed language and *especially* in JavaScript.

- If you have to change an existing test, it's probably not worth it (and not technically a refactoring).

- If you'll be deleting code, it probably **is** worth it.

- If you are unfamiliar with the code, be wary of "cleaning it up". It's too easy to conflate "I don't understand this code" with "this code is poorly designed".

With these guidelines, as well as your own experience, you should be able to get a gut feeling about how a refactoring might make new features more easy to ship.

I call this *responsible refactoring*. Although you don't get to go crazy "improving" your codebase, you do get a clear and simple process to make the code better in a way that has demonstrable, immediate benefits. Think about it next time you are tempted to "clean up" some smelly code.

D

The World's Shortest Language Primers

There's not a lot of source code in this book, but there is some, and I've split it up between Ruby and Java. I've done this for two reasons:

- Java is incredibly popular, with Ruby also garnering significant mindshare.
- I want to underscore the language-agnosticism of the book (I could've just as easily used C# and Python, however I just happen to know Java and Ruby well).

That being said, I don't want you to miss out on the examples, so here's just enough information to understand what's going on in the code examples.

D.1 Ruby

Consider this block of code:

```ruby
class Person
  def initialize(name,birthdate,country)
    @name      = name
    @birthdate = birthdate
    @country   = country
  end

  attr_reader    :name,
                 :birthdate
  attr_accessor :country

  def age
    ((Date.new.to_i - birthdate) / 1000 /
      60 / 24 / 365).to_i
  end

  def minor?
    self.age < 18
  end

  def greet(formal)
    if formal
      "Greetings " +  @name
    else
      "Hey " +  @name
    end
  end
end

p = Person.new("Dave",Date.parse("1973-06-01"),"USA")
p.minor?     # false
p.age        # 39 at time of this writing
p.greet(true) # Greetings Dave
```

- This defines a class named Person from which objects can be built

- `initialize` is the constructor - it is called during object creation

- Instance variables are denoted with the sigil @ and are private - no one outside the class can access them

- `attr_reader` creates a method that returns the value of an instance variable. In other words, you can call `person.name` to get the name of a particular instance of `Person` called `person`

- `attr_accessor` creates both a reader and a writer, allowing you to set the value of an instance variable. In this case, we can change the person's `country` via `person.country = 'UK'`

- Methods are created via `def`. Methods return values are whatever the body of the method evaluates to (explicit returns are not needed). In this case:

  - `age` does a calculation using `birthdate` (which is a method call to the method created by `attr_reader`), and uses `to_i` to convert the floating point result into an integer

  - `minor?` returns a boolean. By convention, Ruby methods that return booleans have a question mark in their name

  - `greet` takes a parameter

- `self` refers to the object itself, so `self.age` means "Call the age method on myself"

- To create instances, you call the method `new` on the class itself. Ruby implements `new` and will call `initialize`

- Methods with no arguments don't require parentheses

- All blocks of code end with `end` - no curly braces

Ruby is a huge amazing language, but this should be enough to allow you to read the few code examples.

D.2   Java

Although Java is ubiquitous, many younger developers have not used Java much (or at all) in their careers. If you've never used it or seen it, it can be daunting because there is a lot of syntax involved. This is both because it is statically typed and because of the many symbols required for various code constructs.

Consider this code:

```java
class Person {
  private String name;
  private Date birthdate;
  private Set<String> countriesLived;

  public Person(String name,
                Date birthdate,
                Set<String> countriesLived) {

    this.name           = name;
    this.birthdate      = birthdate;
    this.countriesLived = countriesLived;
  }

  public String getName() {
    return this.name;
  }

  public Date getBirthdate() {
    return this.birthdate;
  }

  public Set<String> getCountriesLived() {
```

```
    return this.countriesLived;
  }

  public void setCountriesLived(
      Set<String> countriesLived) {
    this.countriesLived = countriesLived;
  }

  public int getAge() {
    return (new Date()).getTime() / 1000 /
      60 / 60 / 24 / 365;
  }

  public String greet(boolean formal) {
    if (formal) {
      return "Greetings " + getName();
    }
    else {
      return "Hey " + getName();
    }
  }
}

Set<String> countries = new Set<String>();
countries.add("USA");
Person person = new Person("Dave",
                           new Date(),
                           countries);
person.getName();    // Dave
person.getAge();     // 0 :)
person.greet(false); // Hey Dave
```

This is roughly the same as our Ruby class, but I added the
concept of "countries lived" to demonstrate a feature of Java
not present in Ruby.

- This defines a class named Person from which objects

can be built

- We define three instance variables that are private. We specify their types and names

- The constructor is the method with the same name as the class that has no return value: `public Person()`. `public` means anyone can use it to create objects

- Arguments require a type that is specified before the argument name. Thus, the first parameter to the constructor is a `String` called `name`

- The third argument's type is `Set<String>`, which means "A `Set` that may only contain instances of `String`". This is called "generics" and is a feature of Java's type system. If you attempt to place a non-`String` into that `Set`, the program won't compile

- `this.` references the object itself, and can disambiguate instance variables from method arguments

- Methods are defined via an access modifier, followed by the return type, followed by the name, and then the arguments, if any

- `setCountriesLived` is public - anyone can call it - returns nothing (`void`) and takes one argument

- `getAge` is public, returns an `int` and takes no arguments

- `if` statements require parens, and code blocks are surrounded by curly braces

Java has gone from a hot new language to the established old guard in just a few years, but it's everywhere and there is a lot of software written for it. It could very well be worth your while to learn it, simply because of the software options it would open up for you.

E

Reading List

The following books and articles heavily influenced me throughout my career and contributed significantly to the contents of this book. They provide much deeper detail into many of the topics covered here and I highly recommend you read them.

5 Essential Phone-Screen Questions by Steve Yegge, published September 2004. Read it online at https://sites.google.com/site/steveyegge2/five-essential-phone-screen-questions

Clean Code by Robert C. Martin, published August 2008. Buy it online at http://www.amazon.com/Clean-Code-Handbook-Software-Craftsmanship/dp/0132350882

The Clean Coder by Robert C. Martin, published May 2011. Buy it online at http://www.amazon.com/The-Clean-Coder-Professional-Programmers/dp/0137081073

Examining Task Engagement/Fogarty05 (full title: "Examining Task Engagement in Sensor-Based Statistical Models of Human Interruptibility") by James Fogerty et. al., published 2005. Read it online at http://www.interruptions.net/literature/Fogarty-CHI05-p331-fogarty.pdf

The Hacker Way by Mark Zuckerberg, published Feb 2012. Read it online at http://www.wired.com/business/2012/02/zuck-letter/

Landing the Tech Job You Love by Andy Lester, published June 2009. Buy it online at http://pragprog.com/book/algh/land-the-tech-job-you-love

On Being a Senior Engineer by John Allspaw, published October 2012. Read it online at http://www.kitchensoap.com/2012/10/25/on-being-a-senior-engineer/

The Passionate Programmer by Chad Fowler, published May 2009. Buy it online at http://pragprog.com/book/cfcar2/the-passionate-programmer

Practices of an Agile Developer by Venkat Subramaniam and Andy Hunt, published April 2006. Buy it online at http://pragprog.com/book/pad/practices-of-an-agile-developer

The Pragmatic Programmer by Dave Thomas and Andy Hunt, published October 1999. Buy it online at http://pragprog.com/book/tpp/the-pragmatic-programmer

Preparing to resume an interrupted task/Trafton02 (full title: "Preparing to resume an interrupted task: effects of prospective goal encoding and retrospective rehearsal") by J. Gregory Trafton et. al., published August 2002. Read it online at http://act-r.psy.cmu.edu/wordpress/wp-content/uploads/2012/12/448preparing.to.resume.pdf

Principles Behind the Agile Manifesto by Beck et. al., published 2001. Read it online at http://agilemanifesto.org/principles.html

Release It! by Michael T. Nygard, published March 2007. Buy it online at http://pragprog.com/book/mnee/release-it

The Twelve-Factor App by Adam Wiggins, published Jan 2012. Read it online at http://www.12factor.net/

About the Author

David Bryant Copeland is a programmer and author. He wrote "Build Awesome Command-Line Applications in Ruby", and has been a professional developer since 1995. He's managed high-performance, high-traffic systems at LivingSocial, helped build the engineering team at Opower, and worked consulting gigs both large and small. Currently, he's Director of Engineering at fashion start-up Stitch Fix, building a platform to change the retail shopping experience.

Made in the USA
Lexington, KY
08 November 2016